# THOR
# SPEAKS!

SECRETS OF THE ANCIENT GODS

# THOR SPEAKS!

## A GUIDE TO THE REALMS BY THE NORSE GOD OF THUNDER

## VICKY ALVEAR SHECTER
## ILLUSTRATIONS BY J. E. LARSON

BOYDS MILLS PRESS
AN IMPRINT OF HIGHLIGHTS
*Honesdale, Pennsylvania*

The author wishes to thank Kevin J. Wanner, PhD, associate professor of Christianity and Comparative Religions at Western Michigan University; Paul Acker, PhD, Professor of Old and Middle English, Old Norse Literature, Critical Thinking and Writing at Saint Louis University; and especially Kim Zarins, PhD, professor of English, Literature and Medieval Studies at California State University, Sacramento, for their help in reviewing the manuscript for this book. Any errors or misinterpretations of Nordic mythology are the author's alone.

Boyds Mills Press, Inc.
An Imprint of Highlights
815 Church Street
Honesdale, Pennsylvania 18431
Printed in the United States of America
ISBN: 978-1-62091-599-8 (print)
ISBN: 978-1-62979-436-5 (e-book)
Library of Congress Control Number: 2015931557
First edition
10 9 8 7 6 5 4 3 2 1
The text of this book is set in Century Schoolbook.
The illustrations are done in pen and ink.

*To Bruce, Matthew, and Aliya*
—VAS

*For my mother, who raised two Norsemen of her own*
—JEL

# CONTENTS

# CAUTION

**T**HOR WANTS YOU TO KNOW that Norse myths and tales varied by region, era, and storyteller. Also, he wants you to be aware that the stories of the Nordic gods and heroes were written hundreds of years after his people stopped worshipping him (he's still mad about that, by the way) and the other Norse gods. Consequently, Thor is convinced that the authors of these stories tried to make the Norse gods (especially him) look a little foolish to strengthen their new religion, Christianity. Which is why he insists that there is absolutely no truth at all to the rumor that he was not the sharpest sword in the armory. To keep your head, you might want to remember that.

# GREETINGS, MORTAL!

**ALLOW ME TO INTRODUCE MYSELF.** I am Thor, the god of protection and strength. The boss of thunder, rain, and lightning. The lord of oaths. The master of good weather. (The master of terrible weather, too, if you make me angry.) And, finally, the god of courage.

That's a lot to manage, I know, but I handle it all easily because I am big and strong and fearless. Also, I have a magic hammer.

Did I mention I was big and strong?

Anyway, some of you may have seen me in comic books or movies, but Hollywood doesn't know the *real* me. I am much cooler than they lead you to believe.

One look at my muscles and most bad guys—usually

ugly trolls and giants—go running in terror. Luckily, most of the time I'm a happy, sunny guy. But if you do something to make me angry, watch out. I will blow up on you—literally. And not just with thunder, either. I will fry you with lightning so hard there will be nothing left but a smoking pile of rags. My rage can shake the earth, make glaciers splinter into shards, and topple great mountains.

But most of the time, I'm a nice guy. Unless you're a giant. Wait, you're not a giant, are you?

## NO GIANTS ALLOWED

The one sure way to get me angry is to put an ugly giant in my path. Seriously, I hate giants. It's my job to keep them away from *Asgard*, where we gods live. So don't even *pretend* to be one of those snarling, knuckle-dragging, hairy beasts. I may lose it and forget you're just a tiny little mortal.

Another thing that makes me angry is any attempt to make me look stupid, which is a favorite pastime of Loki's (a god you'll meet soon). For this reason, I would advise you not to attempt to use fancy words around me or tell me any weird riddles or knock-knock jokes.

It won't go well for you.

## GOAT YOU THERE!

I bet you didn't know that I drive a chariot pulled by goats through the sky. *Goats*, people. Sure, I could've used horses, but how predictable. How boring!

My father, Odin, rides around on an eight-legged steed and I wanted to make my mark by riding through the sky in a different way. Using goats made a statement. It said I was strong. Different. Creative! Okay, goats don't go as fast as eight-legged horses, or even a team of regular horses. And, yeah, they are a tad stubborn. And, true, they smell like the rankest monsters from Hel's domain, our underworld.

But still. They're fun.

And like me, my goats are tough. They're also hard to control, which proves just how strong I am. Some folks say goats are a bit on the dumb side, but this is a complete and total lie. They are just as smart as I am!

To top it all off, my goats are magic, too. If I get hungry and am not in Valhalla (where we feast all the time), all I have to do is slaughter my trusty, horned friends, roast 'em up, and enjoy! When I'm done, I place the bones inside their skins, gently tap my hammer over their hides, and . . . *boom*! They're back, alive and ready to roll. It's the ultimate in travel and takeout!

Anyway. What were we talking about?

Oh, yeah. My awesomeness. In my day, everybody loved me—farmers, herders, partiers, pirates, and warriors—which is why I was the most popular of all the Norse gods. And no, I'm not bragging. I was everyone's "good-buddy" god. Most folks wore tiny hammer charms in my honor for good luck and carved my symbol into all kinds of stones, decorations, and weapons. They buried

"Thor hammers" in graves to protect the dead. They even held up hammers over the heads of newly married couples as a blessing! (Or, as a threat to keep one or both of them from running. Whatever, I don't judge.)

Everybody called on me for protection. After all, if I could protect the gods in Asgard from the terrible giants that wanted to take us down, I could certainly protect you tiny little mortals. Which reminds me—before we go any further, I must warn you: if you don't like blood, you might want to close this book and read stories about pixies and fairies instead. I am not kidding around. My people were famous for their brutality. Vikings attacked, killed, and pillaged their way around most of the medieval world. Nordic myths and legends are pretty brutal, too, filled with evil frost-giants, monster wolves, ravenous dragons, and epic battles of destruction.

If you think you can handle our tales of murder and mayhem, then come along. Step up onto my goat chariot and let's get going. Don't be shy!

*Velkomin* to my world . . .

# THE WILD NORTHMEN

**SEE? IT'S NOT SO BAD** riding behind goats. Well, except for the bumpy ride. Sorry about the smell. Riding behind them after they've gorged on fermented shark—a delicacy in my neck of the woods—was maybe not the best idea. They give the concept of "gas-powered ride" a whole new meaning.

Anyway, as we journey to the mythic realms of my people, you may notice that it's freezing up here. Well, it was—and still is, a great deal of the time—bitterly cold in Scandinavia, which you know today as Sweden, Denmark, Norway, Iceland, and Greenland.

In the days before electricity, it took a special breed of human to survive in the Arctic regions, also known as the world's freezer. The chilling North Sea hammered the coastlines where most of my people settled, trapping them against harsh, craggy ice mountains or prickly forests. In some regions, the land was warmed a bit by the Gulf Stream, allowing my people to grow wheat and barley. In other regions, the ground was too cold to cultivate, so they managed livestock such as cows, goats, and sheep instead. Others made their mark by fishing, trading, and (eventually) pillaging.

Because of the icy mountains and dense forests—especially in places like Norway—getting around on land was often hard. So, my people learned to travel by boat. They became expert boat-makers. They created unique shallow-bottomed ships to sail through the countless *fjords*—long, narrow water inlets between steep mountains—that marked the region. They also became experts at navigating the coastlines around the rough and usually freezing North and Baltic Seas.

Sailing these waters was kind of like what you would get if you crossed a shark with a glacier: killer frostbite. (*Sea* what I did there?) In other words, it was *tough*. Only the hardiest sailors survived it.

During their sea travels, my people learned that lots of folks in Western and Eastern Europe wanted Nordic goods like fur, timber, fish, iron, amber, and pickled herring (mmmm, I eat those by the vat). Throughout most of the fall and winter, it was usually too darn cold to do anything but try to stay warm and survive. By the time spring and summer came around, my people were more than ready to get out and play in the sunshine. In the warmer regions (it's all relative, I know), most began farming as soon as they could work the soil. Others left on boats to make a little money by trading goods.

Still others—some of our more, er, *impatient* young men—wanted to get all the benefits of trading without doing any of the work. Why waste their time, they figured, when they could cut out the middleman—literally, with very sharp swords and axes—and just *take* what they wanted? Sure, pillaging and plundering were a kind of "work," but my raiders considered it something else, too: adventure and fun.

These men came to be known as *Vikings*.

The word comes from the Norse word *vik*, which means "stream, inlet, or small bay." Norse raiders often "parked" their ships in small inlets when they went on the attack, so they became known as "the men who parked their boats in shallow water": Vikings.

Much to the terror of the masses, Vikings swarmed over most of the medieval world. At certain points, Vikings ruled in the British Isles and parts of France. The Norsemen eventually set up kingdoms around the Mediterranean and even in the Middle East. When Vikings came a-callin', most people learned quickly that the only smart thing to do was to go a-runnin'.

Ah, my boys. They made me so proud!

## SEIZING THE BULL BY THE HORNS

**B**efore we go any further, let me clear up one myth: Vikings *did not ever—and I mean, EVER—*wear helmets with horns. Seriously, if you want to see me have a cow, show me a picture of a Viking with a horned helmet. You will suffer from a thunderstorm so severe that you will be left cowering under your bed. No bull.

Though you would never see them in helmets, my people *did* use cow and bull horns for drinking cups. I know what you're thinking—drinking horns? How would that even work? It's not like you can stand them up. Drinks would spill everywhere!

True. And that's exactly why my warriors liked them. See, Vikings had a thing about proving their "manliness." Epic sword fighting was one way. Drinking and eating huge amounts was another. By the way, this was something I excelled in—I was famous for my size and how much I ate and drank. A feast "big enough for Thor" meant it was massive. (Not like I'm bragging or anything, but I did mention that I was big and strong, right?)

Anyway, a "man's man" proved himself by downing

an entire horn—usually filled with mead, a type of fermented drink made with honey—in one giant gulp, many, many times in one sitting. Anything less was considered unmanly. As a result, Viking parties usually ended in *udder* chaos.

## THE FURY OF THE "NORTHMEN"

**V**ikings are so identified with plundering and pillaging that it's sometimes easy to forget that most of my people were ordinary farmers and craftsmen. They spent their days much as you do: hunting bears, skinning wolves, fishing in zero-degree weather, or making reindeer stew. That *is* what you guys do all day, yah?

Some of our guys, though, traveled the seas in search of "easy pickings"—undefended or poorly protected coastal regions. Initially, the easiest targets were monasteries on the coasts of England and Ireland.

Christian monks never imagined that they needed protection from *anybody*. After all, everybody around them was Christian and knew not to mess with their sacred centers of worship. They never counted on invasions from *pagans* (non-Christians). By the time our dragon-headed longships carrying wild-eyed warriors landed on their beaches, it was pretty much all over for them.

According to legend, medieval church leaders everywhere prayed, "From the fury of the Northmen, deliver us, O Lord."

It didn't work.

In just three hundred years, the Vikings spread out over Europe like gamers at a local game shop sale. By the time they were done, they had pretty much cleared out all the goods.

Not only did Vikings attack areas in Ireland, England, France, Scotland, and Russia, but many also settled in these regions as well. Why? Because, well, why not? If the area was good enough to steal from, then it was probably good enough to live in. Plus, the weather must have been a draw. I mean, let's be honest, compared to the freezing lands at home, even rainy England must have seemed like the tropics. So they made their own little cities in the lands they conquered.

From the time the Northmen began pillaging and settling new lands, to when the Scandinavians converted to Christianity, is called "The Viking Age."

I myself like to think of it as "The Awesome Times."

## TOUGH MYTHS FOR TOUGH PEOPLE

Our creation story began with an epic World-Wrestling-Entertainment-like fight between ice and fire. When the two smacked into each other, a troll-like ice-giant was created. Life emerged from this giant's *sweaty armpit.* I am not kidding. Here's the story:

*Ice from Niflheim in the North and fire from the South crashed together in a vast pit of nothingness. Amidst the hissing and popping of the great collision, some of the ice melted, creating* Ymir, *the first of the giants and the father of all evil creatures.*

*More ice melted, from which an enormous cow emerged. Her milk nourished the giant. She nourished herself on a huge salt lick. As she licked and licked, a god emerged from the salt-rock. His name was* Buri.

*Ymir the ice-giant began to sweat, and from his stinky armpit emerged two giants—one male, one female These giants had many, many terrible giant children. Meanwhile, Buri, the god who had emerged from the salt lick, had a mighty son, and they faced off against the evil giants. Neither side won. It was a draw between good and evil. Eventually, Buri's son married a giantess and they had several sons who were bigger and stronger than all the other gods that came before and after. One of these sons was* Odin.

*Odin and his brothers killed the first evil frost-giant, Ymir. All of the giants except two died in the flood of Ymir's blood. From those two survivors descended all the evil and awful ice-, frost-, storm-, and mountain-giants that hounded both gods and* men. The giants and Odin's team of good-guy gods remained mortal enemies.

Meanwhile, Odin created the world from the slain giant's body—Ymir's blood became the vast oceans, his bones became mountains, and his hair spiked into trees. His muscles and skin melted into the soil and earth, his teeth moldered into rocks and pebbles. His skull formed the vault of the sky. While Odin was busy, maggots crawled out of Ymir's dead body; these became dwarves. Odin made four of these little guys hold up the corners of the sky. He then divided creation into nine separate realms within three major "worlds"—Niflheim, the lower regions of all things darkly dangerous; Midgard, or Middle Earth, for humans; and Asgard, for all the gods.

Below the earth lived the icy dark forces of chaos from which the world emerged. This chaos also contained the world of the dead, ruled by the dark goddess Hel. This was Niflheim.

The frost-giant's eyelashes formed Midgard, for the humans. Odin and his brothers created humans when they stumbled across two fallen trees. They fashioned a man and a woman out of the wood. Odin breathed life into them and the brothers gave them intelligence and hearts. Odin then took the dead giant's eyebrows and formed a fence to protect humans from the remaining frost-giants. He made the dwarves live and work under the ground in Midgard *because of their maggoty origins. They became expert smiths and craftsmen, creating many powerful and magical tools.*

*Finally, in the upper regions above Middle Earth, the gods made a home for themselves in Asgard. Odin connected Asgard to Midgard with a giant rainbow bridge called Bifrost, protected by one of his sons.*

So there you have it. Our creation myth involved murder, blood, maggots, armpit funk, and dangerous ice- and frost-giants—who, in a way, represented the hardships of living in the far North. Only the hardiest of people survived in old Scandinavia. And since I'm the hardiest of all the gods, it's no wonder they loved me best!

## THE TREE OF LIFE

Yggdrasill (*igg*-dra-sill), the great ash tree of life, spans the nine worlds of the Nordic cosmos, as you can see from the map on the next page. Each root of the great tree runs through each of the three main realms: Asgard for the gods, Midgard for the mortals, and Niflheim for the underworld. I will take you on a personal tour of each.

We'll start our tour of the Nordic realms with the lower worlds, because we Vikings are *fearless*. We can handle anything that might come after us in Niflheim, right? Just be sure to hang on tight to this chariot, because if you fall out and get lost down

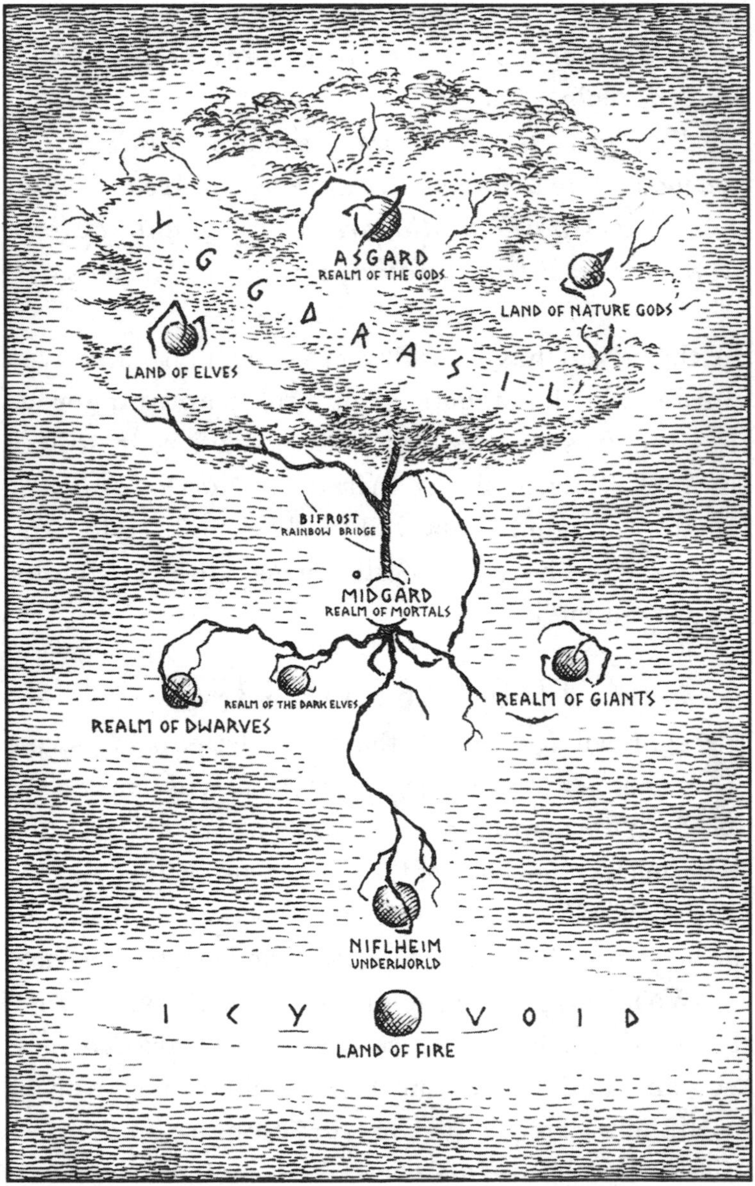

YGGDRASIL

ASGARD
REALM OF THE GODS

LAND OF NATURE GODS

LAND OF ELVES

BIFROST
RAINBOW BRIDGE

MIDGARD
REALM OF MORTALS

REALM OF THE DARK ELVES

REALM OF DWARVES

REALM OF GIANTS

NIFLHEIM
UNDERWORLD

I C Y     V O I D
LAND OF FIRE

there, you're on your own. You especially don't want to tumble out where you could get nabbed by a frost-giant, swallowed by the enormous dragon-serpent nibbling at the great tree's roots, or lose yourself in Hel's domain, the bleak world of the dead.

Oh, look! Loki is down there. Let's fly down to the roots of Yggdrasill and have a little chat with him, shall we?

# LOKI AND THE DARK SIDE

**DESPITE WHAT HOLLYWOOD MOVIES,** video games, and comic books say, Loki—the god of fire, trickery, and mischief—is *not* my brother. He is more of a step-uncle. See, he and my dad, Odin, became blood brothers, which means they probably mixed their blood and declared they were BFFs (brother-friends forever). No one knows why they did this, but I for one am sure Dad regrets it on the regular.

Loki's dad was a frost-giant, but thanks to my father's bloody declaration, Loki lived with us in Asgard as if he'd been born one of us gods. I have often asked our Allfather, "Really, Dad? Why in the name of Bifrost would you make him *family*?" He has never really answered me, except to mutter that you can't enjoy the good without suffering the bad. Whatever *that* means.

Anyway, I've already warned the trickster god that he is not allowed to play his little tricks on you humans. (Trust me—you'd never survive them.) Still, you might want to be careful around him. Do not agree to *any* of his offers. And don't fall for the "Who, me?" face he's perfected. He may look innocent, but he's more dangerous than a wolf who has just scented blood.

Now, go on. Don't drag your feet. Say hello to the god of mischief. . . .

# LOKI

**A**h, welcome, young mortals. I am not sure what my dear, lovable, oafish nephew has said about me, but let me assure you—I am in no way evil and I would never harm you. Unless I get bored, which, as Thor well knows, happens easily. Very easily.

Some folks like to paint me as a mean trickster, but I'm really not. It's just that I love to get a rise out of my puffed-up, overly proud family. And annoying and making fun of Thor is one of my favorite pastimes. Just because.

You should know, too, by the way, that I'm responsible for Thor's magic hammer. Don't roll your eyes, thunderboy. You know it's true. Here's how it happened.

Thor was out battling giants when I saw his beautiful wife, Sif, moping for him. I was in no way jealous, but seriously? I mean, how did that big lug get *such a lovely and devoted wife?*

*Sif's long golden hair cascaded around her like a shining waterfall. Wouldn't it be funny, I thought, if she suddenly didn't have all that hair? So I waited until she was asleep, snuck into her palace bedroom, and cut it all off. I was giggling so hard, I almost gave myself away!*

*Sif, however, did not think it was funny at all. When she awoke and saw that her hair was gone, she cried. Thor returned home and Sif hid from him. He flew into a rage when he saw what had happened to her and complained to Odin and the council of the gods. He and everybody else blamed me, of course.*

*"I will kill Loki!" Thor thundered.*

*Odin stopped him from slaying me by making me promise to restore Sif's beautiful hair. What choice did I have? I agreed.*

*So I went down the rainbow bridge—Bifrost— to make an appeal to the dwarves, because they are the best craftsmen and smiths in all our realms. The underground world of the dwarves is dark and smoky because they spend all their time either mining for metals or smithing the metals into wondrous creations. I went deep underground and watched the little men work as they tried to impress me. One dwarf made a spear so fine and true, it would never miss its mark, no matter who threw it. Another made a boat that could navigate any sea but then folded up again and again until it fit in your wallet. I knew I had to have those two* things, so I sweet-talked the dwarves, convincing them they would be the heroes of Asgard if only they let me have what they'd just created.

Then I spied a bar of pure gold and flattered them some more, wondering out loud if any of them had the talent to take that gold bar and turn it into golden threads as fine and as beautiful as Sif's hair. They all jumped at the chance to prove that they could do it. With their tiny hammers, they worked the gold into a mass of silken threads. When they finished, I again convinced them to let me have their creation.

In my excitement, I praised the dwarves as the most talented in all the realms. But one evil dwarf didn't like the sound of that.

"They may be good," he said, "but they are not as good as my brother, Sindri."

The other dwarves scoffed angrily.

"I will bet you," I said, "that your brother cannot make three things to equal this hair, ship, and spear that these dwarves have just made."

"Not only can Sindri equal them, but he can best them," the dwarf, named Brokkr, promised.

"Ha!" I laughed.

"Would you bet your head on that?" Brokkr asked.

"Of course!" I said, confidently. After all, the stuff I had in my hands was unbeatable! I should've gotten nervous when the dwarf gave me an evil smile. Off we went to the brother-dwarf's forge.

I hovered outside the door and spied through a crack.

"I will easily make things that will surpass what the others made," Sindri boasted. "But I will need your help, brother. You must keep the fire extra-hot by working the bellows."

Brokkr agreed to help.

Once the furnace was roaring and red-hot, Sindri threw into it the skin of a pig and, before leaving the smithy, told his brother he must keep the fire going at all costs. Brokkr put everything he had into working the bellows.

This gave me an idea. I turned myself into a gadfly, flew into the room, and stung Brokkr's hand. I figured he'd jump back and stop feeding the fire. But he ignored me! He stopped the bellows only when Sindri returned. From the fire, Sindri pulled a live golden boar whose body brightened the room like a magic lamp. That's when I started to worry.

Then Sindri threw a gold bar into the forge and again instructed Brokkr to work the bellows like a madman. Still in the form of a gadfly, I bit him hard on the neck. No reaction. When Sindri returned, he pulled out a magic golden arm ring.

Then he threw an iron bar into the fire and again told his brother to keep the fire super-hot. This time, I had to stop Brokkr from pumping the bellows, so I flew to his forehead and bit so hard I drew blood. Still the *dwarf kept pumping with tremendous power. A bit of the blood from his forehead dripped down into his eye, and he paused for one second to wipe it away, then continued working the bellows.*

*Sindri returned and pulled out of the fire a powerful hammer. Immediately, he saw that the handle was shorter than it should've been, thanks to that one moment Brokkr had paused to wipe his eye.*

*Still, Sindri was pleased. The battle hammer was a mighty impressive weapon. We took all of the gifts up to Asgard so the gods could vote on which of the gifts were finer.*

*With a bow, I gave the cap of golden hair to Thor, who placed it on his wife's head. The gold immediately rooted into her scalp and became her hair, even more beautiful than before. To Frey, the god of agriculture and fertility, I gave the unsinkable ship that folded up to fit in a pocket. He loved it. To Odin, I presented the golden spear. Odin agreed it was a perfect weapon.*

I got this, *I thought to myself.* I will definitely win the bet.

*But then Sindri stepped up. He gave Odin the golden arm ring and pronounced that on the ninth night he wore it, eight rings just like it would fall out of the original, so that after a year, he would have a seemingly endless—and endlessly refilling—treasure. Odin thought it wonderful and placed it on his arm.*

The dwarf then gave the golden boar to Frey, telling him that not only would the magical beast pull his chariot, but its golden bristles would illuminate every dark place like a lamp. Frey was thrilled. I began to seriously get nervous then. I mean, who could compete with a glow-in-the-dark pig lamp/chariot?

Finally, the dwarf put the mighty hammer called Mjöllnir (mee-*uhl*-neer) *in Thor's hands.* "No matter how far you throw it, it will always return to you," he said. "Only you have the strength to wield it in protection of the gods."

Thor grinned and immediately began hurling the weapon around the hall, forcing everyone to duck lest they lose their heads.

I was most definitely worried by this point.

Odin and the other gods made their pronouncement—all the gifts were spectacular, but Thor's hammer edged out the others. I had lost.

Brokkr laughed and clapped. "Now your head is mine," he crowed, pulling out his knife.

Thinking fast, I said, "Wait! I agreed you could have my head, but I did not say you could take any part of my neck. And since you can't take my head without taking some of my neck, you're out of luck."

At this, the gods laughed at my brilliance. They sided with me against the dwarf.

"It's true," Odin told the dwarf. "He has outwitted you. You cannot have his head!"

Brokkr stomped away in a fury and I got the credit

*for making Thor's hammer. Couldn't have arranged it better myself!*

Wait, you left out the best part of the story, Loki! Brokkr was so mad about being cheated out of your head, he grabbed a needle and thread, and before you could stop him, he sewed your mouth shut before disappearing. Honestly, the look on your face when he did it was priceless. I laughed so hard I accidentally made a glacier fall into the sea.

Oh, wait. Loki has disappeared. Huh. Maybe making Loki angry while you guys are down here wasn't the best idea I've ever had. Oh, well. I got your back, kid.

Loki failed to mention that in addition to my magic hammer, I also own *Megingjardar* (*may*-in-gee-yarth-are), a magic belt of power. Whenever I put it on, my strength doubles. Plus, I also have a pair of magic iron gloves called *Járngreiper* (*Jarn*-gripper), which give me greater purchase on my hammer's short handle.

Still, you should know that I don't actually *need* these power tools. I mean, I'm already super-strong. But I'm not going to lie—using them is a *blast*! And no, I won't let you borrow them. Ever. Seriously, stop asking.

Let's meet Loki's children instead. Now, you'd think the god of mischief would have fun-lovin' kids, but that is not the case. At all. One of his kids is a giant serpent bent on destroying the world. Another is the queen of death—literally—who reigns over the land of the dead. And the third is a giant fearsome wolf who will ultimately destroy all of us.

I guess the fruit really doesn't fall far from the tree.

## BEWARE THE SCARY DRAGON

**A**s we explore the worlds under Yggdrasill, the great ash tree of life, keep an eye out for the dragon named *Nidhogg*. This dragon-serpent is bent on destroying the very roots of the world. But Nidhogg doesn't just chew on the tree of life. He also chews up the corpses of the dead.

Nice, eh?

So, if you think my goats have bad breath, you definitely do not want to get near Nidhogg's mouth. The stench can melt the eyebrows and nose-hairs right off your face. As we pass by him, you'd better act lively, too. You know he is watching us with those beady reptile eyes. We wouldn't want him to mistake you for newly dead and make you his latest chew toy.

Nidhogg gets his snack corpses from Hel, Loki's daughter. She rules over the land of the dead. Hel is, by the way, where we get the English word *hell*. And in the Viking era, telling someone to "Go to Hel" meant "Go die!"

Since we're already down here, let's say hi to Hel.

# HEL'S HALL

**A**ccording to my people, warriors who died in combat—or men who died fighting for their honor in single combat—went to *Valhalla*, my father's hall in the upper world of Asgard. Everybody else went to Hel. Literally. Women, children, the old, the sick, the accident-prone—anyone who did not die a warrior's death found their way here.

Oh, look. She must have heard us talking about her. That creature emerging from the thick blackness? That's Hel.

Don't be alarmed by her hag-like looks. Some legends say she's blue—as in, blue like a corpse—but others say she most often shows up as she looks now: half a withering corpse, half as pale as death. You have to admit, whatever half you settle upon, she's full-on scary.

Not like I'm frightened. In the least. I swear.

Anyway, Hel's world is clammy, miserable, and pitch-dark. I can barely see you, so stay close. And all those downcast gray people walking about? They're the dead. Sadly, they don't have anything to do except mope.

Hel is not a place of punishment, like some afterworlds. For the folks here, their only "crime" was not dying a hero's death on the battlefield. And for that horrible, horrible outrage, they pay with eternal misery.

See, for Vikings, violence and war were considered great things—if you won the battle and lived, you got a little richer. If you lost the battle and died, you went to Odin's hall, Valhalla, and partied every night with the Allfather. Plus, for fun and giggles, they constantly battled each other in preparation for the big battle at the end of time. See, so even if you died with an ax in your head, it was all win-win!

My people had a very interesting concept of death. If a baby was named after a dead person, they believed the baby could inherit an actual part of that person, usually their luck, bad or good. They could also have the spirit of a dead animal born into them, which showed up in the way they acted. So, someone could be bear-like, wolf-like, or (if they ate a lot!) pig-like.

## SNAKE-HATING MR. HAIRYPANTS

As expected, the place is teeming with the sick and the old, and with women and children. And yet, if you look closely, you'll find some men dressed in battle gear down here. Surprised? Don't be. Sadly, some warriors here made the terrible mistake of not dying in battle. They had the bad luck to get old or sick. And they are a very unhappy bunch.

Let's meet some of them:

**Ragnar Lodbrook (a.k.a. Ragnar "Hairypants"):** Why was he called "Hairypants?" Well, either his legs were so hairy they looked like pants, or (more likely) he wore pants that looked as though they were made of hair.

Anyway, he's the guy in the corner tying snakes into knots. He is not happy about being down here, especially since he successfully attacked many regions in France and England. So why didn't he go to Valhalla? Because he was captured on a raid in England and died—not in battle, but in prison, in a pit of snakes. According to legend, he died bravely. Still, no battlefield death, no Valhalla. Too bad. So sad.

**Hastein:** That confused-looking Viking asking everyone for directions was actually one of the most formidable Vikings of his era. Hastein raided in England, France, and North Africa. Once he went to Italy, hoping to sack Rome, the powerful center of Christianity at the time. When he landed on the Italian coast, he came up with a trick to get inside the city gates. He pretended to be dying and was brought in on a stretcher, his men begging the priests to give him last rites. When the priests and officials surrounded him, he jumped up and attacked! At some point, he learned he wasn't in Rome at all, but in a city called Luna. He was so mad at his own mistake that he attacked the city even more savagely. So why is he in Hel? Poor dude died of old age. Next time, hopefully, he'll learn to read a map—*and* the fine print on making it to Valhalla.

**Harald Fairhair:** The dude brushing his long mane is golden-haired Harald. He united Norway after he fell in love with a girl who claimed she would marry him only if he became king of "all Norway." So, he swore not to cut his hair until he did so. It took him ten years to become king and during that time he was called "Shaggy Harald" or "Shockhead Harald." Once he accomplished his goal and won the girl, he finally combed his hair and got a little trim. The tragedy is, of course, that this great hero died of old age! I mean, *dude.* The Viking way was to be remembered for your violence on the battlefield, not your pretty hair!

**Rollo:** The guy in the corner constantly flipping that confused old man onto his back is Rollo, who invaded France and eventually became king of what was known as Normandy. He is demonstrating (for the fifteen-billionth time, I might add), how he dissed the king of France. During a peace treaty meeting between Rollo and King Charles, the king demanded Rollo kiss his foot to seal the deal. Rollo refused to bend a knee to anyone. He was a Viking conqueror after all! When the king insisted, Rollo made one of his men do it. But his underling lifted the king's foot so high that Charles fell backward in a most undignified fashion. All the Vikings laughed and laughed at this. Poor dude died as an old, old man rather than a warrior, so he's stuck down here.

**Leif Erikson:** See that empty chair with an oar placed over it? That's Leif's spot. He's not down here because he converted to Christianity and went somewhere else after death. However, we like to remember the son of Erik the Red here because he was the first European to land in North America, nearly five hundred years before Christopher Columbus. He did not die in battle so if he had continued believing in the Norse gods, he would've been down here with the rest of the old timers. Rules are rules!

The line of warriors who sadly grew old and died away from the battlefield is getting pretty long, so let's turn our attention to somebody more interesting. See that guy looking downcast in the chair of honor next to Hel? He's Baldur, one of my own brothers.

## PRETTY BOY BLUE

Everybody loved Baldur, my golden-haired brother made of light and virtue. He was known as The Shining One, the god of goodness, innocence, and forgiveness. One god, though, didn't like Baldur at all. Care to guess who that might be? Let me give you a hint—he's a wily, scheming, backstabbing, liar god whose name begins with *L*.

*Baldur, the shining god of joy and courage, began having dark dreams of death. Odin went down to Hel's place to speak to a dead prophetess to find out why he had such dreams. She was busy helping Hel prepare for a festival to welcome a very important person who would soon join them down there. Odin's heart sunk when she told him they were expecting his own son, Baldur.*

*Back in Asgard, he told his fellow gods about the prophecy. Frigg, Baldur's mother, was heartbroken and determined to save her beloved son. She went to every living thing in the cosmos and extracted a promise that they would never hurt the golden god.*

*Once Baldur's safety was secured, the gods made a game of throwing rocks, spears, and knives at him. Nothing ever hurt him so it became a great party game. Good-natured Baldur endured it.*

*Loki, however, was suspicious. Was it really possible to convince everything in the world to not hurt Baldur? So he disguised himself as a hag and went to Frigg. "So all things everywhere promised not to harm Baldur?" he asked Baldur's mother.*

*"Yes," she said.*

*"Everything? Are you sure?"*

*Frigg paused. "Well, except for mistletoe. That little*

plant is so small and harmless, I figured there was no point in asking it."

Loki slithered away and immediately went in search of the plant. When he found it, he secretly brought it back to Asgard and made a spear tip from it. When all the gods were together once again hurling sharp weapons at Baldur, Loki saw his chance.

He approached the blind god Hod and said, "Don't you feel left out? Wouldn't you like to play this game proving Baldur's invincibility?"

"It would be fun to throw something at him," Hod agreed.

"Here, take this," Loki said, grabbing the blind god's hand and wrapping it around the mistletoe spear. "I'll guide your hand."

To everyone's dismay, the spear went through Baldur's heart, killing him instantly. Down to the place of the dead he went.

Odin and Frigg were despondent. They sent a messenger to Hel, begging her to return his life. The whole world grieved over the loss of Baldur, they told her.

Normally, Hel would never consider relinquishing her rights to one of the dead, but she finally offered one chance. "If everyone and everything weeps for him, then I will let him go and live," Hel said. "But if only one does not, he stays with me."

The gods went to every living thing, confirming that they still wept for the beautiful "Good One." All things *still grieved for Baldur. One day, they came upon a hag with blackened teeth and asked her if she still grieved. "I do not weep for Baldur," the hag spat. "Let Hel keep him." The hag, of course, was Loki in disguise. Because of Loki's words, Hel would not release Baldur. The great sadness this caused was but one of the signs that the end of times—Ragnarök—was on the horizon.*

To honor Baldur's death, we held a Viking funeral for him. We placed his body on a boat, set it ablaze, and watched as it drifted away from the shore of the living. We gave many of our heroes similar burials.

Still, we gods never forgot the heartlessness of Loki's crime and we banded together to punish him. Like a little coward, he ran away. To escape our wrath, he turned himself into a salmon and hid under a waterfall. But I, Thor, caught him by the tail (which is why salmon tails are so slender, by the way), threw him into a cave as he transformed into his god-form, and imprisoned him there for a long time.

It was the least we could do for poor Baldur.

But all this talk about Hel is bringing me down. Let's make like bats and fly out of here once and for all. It's time to move on to Midgard, the realm of you puny mortals.

# WELCOME TO MIDDLE EARTH

**IF DRAGONS, GIANTS,** magic rings, elves, and Middle Earth sound familiar to you, it's because a guy named J. R. R. Tolkien wrote a bunch of fantasy novels based on Norse myths. You may have heard of *The Hobbit* and *The Lord of the Rings* or seen the movies. (Read the books first; they're *wayyyy* better.) In Tolkien's stories, dragons, dwarves, elves, kings of Middle Earth, and all manner of interesting characters, such as an old wandering wizard (Gandalf, based on Odin) and men who can turn into bears, show up. Some people say Tolkien stole outright from our myths and legends.

Others say he merely turned to us for "inspiration." Me? I say he acted just like a Viking: he "pillaged" our stories. He pounced on our legends and snatched their riches for his own excellent creations. That makes him one of the best Vikings of all—a successful plunderer!

I think we should have a feast in his honor. Cow horns of juice for everyone!

Anyway, if you turn back to the map of the world tree, you'll see that Midgard, or Middle Earth, where you humans live, is our next stop.

But, beware, young mortal, you are not alone in Middle Earth!

## DANGER ALL AROUND US

As we fly into Midgard on my goat-chariot, beware evil rock-giants, raging frost-giants, and dwarves. My people believed these evils were invisible to humans. But don't worry, I have excellent supernatural vision, and I'll protect you from their terribleness.

So old are these Nordic beliefs in scary invisible creatures that, even today, in Iceland, roads will not be built over certain fields or lava formations to avoid disturbing the elves or the "hidden people" within the rocks. And everyone knows bad things happen when elves are displaced and disturbed. Elves are fiercely territorial and will take their revenge by making people get into accidents, fall off their bulldozers, get sick, or injure themselves.

Most modern Icelanders say they don't *really* believe in elves or dwarves, but plans for more than one road or building project have been abandoned and the blame put on elves. Just saying.

Iceland was settled in the late ninth century by Vikings who had run afoul of King Harald Fairhair of Norway (we met Goldilocks in Hel's domain, if you recall). Its unique landscape—everything from craggy rock mountains to strange patches of earth roiling with steam—lent itself to stories about frost-giants, storm-giants, and lava monsters. And as in most of Scandinavia when big storms hit, it probably felt like a giant was actually stomping around in a rage.

At the same time, Icelandic volcanoes erupt throughout what seems like a frozen wasteland. You haven't seen anything until you've seen lava spewing from an ice mountain: fire and ice battling it out, just like in our creation story.

Plus, most of my people in the other Nordic settlements lived on the coasts of very cold and rough oceans, including the North Atlantic and the Baltic Seas. Killer waves, flooding, and drowning were very real dangers. And who surrounded all those oceanic evils? A child of Loki, of course—a ravenous evil serpent named *Jörmungandr* (*your*-mun-gander), also known as the Midgard Serpent, that will destroy us all at *Ragnarök*, the terrible day we good guy gods face off with the forces of evil.

I don't know why my father puts up with that wily father-of-a-snake Loki. He is seriously bad news.

# THE SERPENT
# SURROUNDING THE WORLD

**W**hen Odin first saw the monstrosity Loki had spawned, he picked up the evil serpent and heaved it way out into the oceans. You should have seen that snake writhing and twisting in the air! What a sight.

Unfortunately, this infuriated Jörmungandr. He grew and grew until he circled the entire earth. When he saw the end of his tail, he attacked it as if it were Odin and would not let go.

According to the sagas of old, I'm destined to defeat that snake at the great end-of-the-world battle. That's right—*me*! No one else is capable of taking on that monster, not even Odin.

Sadly, before it dies, the snake will spew its supernatural venom all over me. I will walk nine paces before I collapse and die.

I don't like this "destiny" for obvious reasons. In fact, it's making me really angry. Where's my hammer? Every time I think about that snake, I want to create a storm so big, your little mortal newscasters will call it things like the "storm of the decade" or the "stormpocalypse."

But I won't. For now. Instead, I'll tell you the two stories about me and that horrible, slimy serpent of the world:

# THE DAY I CAPTURED THE SERPENT

**T**his is everyone's favorite story, by the way. My people captured this tale on many stone carvings and, later, in illuminated (painted) manuscripts.

*One day, I decided to dress like a mortal and visit the giant Hymir. He was friendly enough. The next morning, Hymir prepared to go deep-sea fishing.*

*"I want to come, too!" I yelled up at him.*

*The giant shook his massive head. "You're too little! Besides, it will take so long to get to my fishing spot, you will either catch cold or freeze."*

*"No way," I said. "I can row hard. I can tell you that it's not going to be me who gets tired of rowing first."*

*The giant's deep laughter almost caused an avalanche. Honestly, I wanted to take my magic hammer and bop him one, but I controlled myself.*

*Finally, Hymir agreed and told me to get my own bait. I saw a herd of oxen, picked out the biggest, lopped off its head, and climbed aboard the ship. Together we rowed way, way out to sea. All the while, the giant marveled at my strength and endurance.*

*The giant wanted to stop, but I said, "No, I'm not tired." I showed him! Finally, Hymir said, "If we don't stop soon, we'll be risking our lives because we'll be near the Midgard Serpent," which, of course, made me* want to row even farther.

Finally, we stopped. I made a strong fishing line, baited the ox-head on my hook, and flung the head overboard. Soon enough, the serpent lunged for it, the hook piercing all the way through the roof of its mouth.

And boy was the serpent mad! I had to harness all my divine strength to control it as it thrashed, creating gigantic waves. I grew to my huge divine shape, my heels plunged right through the boat's bottom, and I pushed them against the seabed as I fought to control the mad beast.

I drew the serpent up from the sea and glared at it, eye to eye. That creature had the nerve to burp poison in my face! Oh, man—I was red with rage. I grabbed Mjöllnir, my magic hammer, and was about to bash its head in, but the terrified giant cut my fishing line, releasing the beast. I howled and threw my hammer at the serpent's head, but it had already disappeared deep under the water.

I was so furious with Hymir for cutting the line, I boxed his ears with the hammer when it returned to me. The giant fell face-first into the water. I then waded all the way back to shore, grumbling about the stupid giant with his stupid knife that kept me from destroying the stupid beast that wants to destroy us all.

# THE DAY A GIANT TRICKED ME

Let's just say that I do not care for this giant or his little tricks. Pretending a cat is a serpent? Even worse.

*One day, Loki, a servant, and I journeyed to the land of the giants. When the sky grew dark, we found a huge abandoned hall and settled in for the night. But just as we dropped off, the earth shook and we heard a terrible groaning and rumbling. We jumped up in alarm, unable to figure out the cause of the frightful sound. I stood guard outside the hall with my magic hammer all night long as the terrible sounds continued. In the morning, we left our sanctuary and saw a giant nearby, sound asleep and snoring. I then understood the terrible sounds. I put on my belt of strength to fight the monster, but it suddenly awoke and sprung to its feet.*

*Before I could attack, the giant asked, "Did you move my glove?" He reached down and held it up, and I realized that we hadn't spent the night in a hall at all, but in the thumb opening of the giant's glove!*

*The giant allowed us to accompany him deeper into giant-land, and that night the snoring was even worse. I grabbed my magic hammer and hit him in the middle of his head to make him stop. The giant snorted and murmured, "Did a leaf fall on my head?"*

*My mouth dropped open. The giant fell back asleep,*

*snoring so loudly the forest shook! Even angrier, I wound up and hit him again with my hammer. He awoke and asked, "Did an acorn drop from the tree?" He began snoring again.*

*I was so angry I could barely speak, so I mustered all my great strength, and when the giant snored again, I wound up and crashed my magic hammer into his temple. The giant awoke and said, "Did a bird poop on my face?"*

*Thankfully, the giant separated from us and went on his merry way. We set off to see the giant-king. When we arrived, the king was less than welcoming.*

*"You can stay here," the king of giants intoned, "only if you have a special skill."*

*"I can out-eat all the giants here," cried Loki.*

*I rolled my eyes because, seriously? String bean Loki could never keep up with me on the eating front. Still, I didn't say anything since we were both quite hungry. A trench full of roasted meat was set up. Loki and a giant set off chomping on each end of the trench and finally met in the middle. Loki thought he'd won because he'd left only the bones. However, the king claimed the giant won because he'd eaten the meat, the bones, and the trench!*

*My servant, a boy about your age, told the giant-king that he could run faster than any of his men. They held the races, and our man lost three different times.*

*Such amateurs. I would show them how it was done.*

"I can outdrink all of you!" I cried.

The giant-king brought out an enormous drinking horn. "If you drink it in one draft, you win," he said. "Or if you drink it in two—or even three!"

No problem, I thought. I put my mouth to that horn and chug-a-lugged like nobody's business. But when I drank so much that I lost my breath, I removed the cup and saw that hardly any of the drink was gone. I drank deeply again. The level of liquid did not move. For a third time, I drank with the same result.

"What kind of trickery is this?" I roared. I could feel my face growing red, fingers itching for my magic hammer. These giants were big, but this was ridiculous! "I will fight any one of you!" I cried.

The king said, "Only if you can lift that large cat over there."

Lift up a kitty cat? Please. I went over to the creature and lifted with all my might—which is considerable, I must say—fully expecting "Fluffy" to go flying into the air. To my amazement, it barely budged. Now I was getting really mad.

Again and again, I tried, using all my godly strength, but I could not lift the cat. The best I could do was to lift its paw.

Panting with rage, I told the king I had to fight someone. "Sure," he said, and sent in an old woman.

I could not believe the insult! I lunged at the old crone but, like the cat, she didn't budge. With her gnarled fingers, she somehow threw me off balance when I tried again.

"Cheater!" I yelled. "You are using trickery to make us lose!" I was about to come after the king, but he suddenly said, "We have very comfy rooms for you to sleep in tonight."

Oh. Well, that stopped me cold. I mean, I love to fight and eat and drink, but I also love a good long snooze.

"Fine," I said, and we set off to sleep.

In the morning, the giant-king gave us a fine breakfast. Good food, I should remind you, always takes the edge off my temper. My anger was like the memory of thunder—it had long rumbled away.

The king escorted us outside his kingdom and then turned to us. "I have a confession," he began. "You didn't lose the contests we held for you—you fought against spells and illusions."

"What?" I asked.

"Loki didn't lose the eating contest to a giant—he lost to a wildfire that consumes everything in its path. Your companion was not slower than the giant he raced—he actually ran against the speed of thought, which can never be beaten."

"And what about me?" I asked. "What did I compete against?"

"You were drinking the sea," the giant said. "No one would've been able to drink it all in one gulp. However, you deeply impressed us because sea levels dropped by *several feet after your attempt. We now call it the ebb tide.*

*"As for the cat, it was actually Jörmungandr, the enormous serpent that surrounds the world. When you picked up the 'cat's' paw, you actually lifted the serpent's middle so high, only its tail and head continued touching the ground. This also amazed us.*

*"Finally," the king continued, "you didn't fight an old crone. She was an illusion like all the others. You lost to old age itself, which no one defeats."*

*Okay, a little part of me was relieved I hadn't actually been defeated in all those contests, but still—I was angry. No one makes a fool of Thor. No one! I raised my hammer, ready to strike down that big deceiver when he suddenly turned into mist. I turned to destroy his hall, but it, too, disappeared.*

*In the end, my rage had no outlet so I just shrugged and headed for home in Asgard. There would be more food and drink there, I reminded myself. And that always made me happy.*

# SNAKE-Y ATTACKS
# AND DRAGON SHIPS

**MIDGARD MORTALS**—a.k.a. my people—both admired and feared snakes and serpents. No surprise, then, that they built all kinds of excellent ships named after them.

Building boats of all sizes and for all uses—from island hopping to fishing—became our specialty. Traders used sturdy, broad-beamed ships to carry their goods. My water warriors, though, preferred sleek longships that could easily navigate both open seas and coastal waters.

One type of attack—a *strandhogg* or flash raid—could never have taken place without the kind of ship that allowed quick movement and fast retreat. The best ships for this kind of attack were called *snekkja,* or snakes, because they were long and sleek, and they struck hard and fast. Snekkja had shallow bottoms, which allowed them to sail far onto the shore and up shallow fjords or rivers without being run aground.

However, no other ship struck more fear into the hearts of coastal people than the Viking dragon ships. Called *dreki* (dragons), the prows of these enormous ships were often carved and painted with terrifying dragon heads. Brightly striped sails billowed behind. Shining shields hung from the ship's sides while as many as eighty oarsmen cut through the water in attack mode. Dragon ships could carry up to sixty armed Vikings ready for battle. Imagine a fleet of them!

Longships had downsides, though. Without benches, men had to bring their own sea chests to sit on. There were no awnings or covers, so if it rained, the men got deeply and thoroughly soaked. Particularly in the cold North Sea, this meant they could stay cold and wet for days on end. Like our lands, navigating our seas required tough men who didn't wilt under difficult circumstances.

And no one was tougher and scarier than our very own "berserkers."

# WILD AND CRAZY FIGHTERS

A special class of warrior made everyone around them quake with fear. These men belonged to a cult celebrating Odin, the god of warriors and war. They'd whip themselves into a frenzy of rage and violence, sometimes biting their own shields as they howled and roared in preparation for their attack.

Many a monk wet his robes at the mere sight of them!

Unleashed on the battlefield, these men went "berserk" with violence, killing anything that moved. We called them "berserkers," which is where you get the word *berserk*, which means acting wild, crazy, and out-of-control.

Our berserkers often acted like mad wolves or bears. Some even wore shirts made of bearskins. With their wild howling and barking and their crazy-eyed rage, they instilled terror in everyone—even other Vikings!

So fearless and full of rage did berserkers seem in battle, rumors swirled that they were immune to attack. Not true. Likely, the fighting produced an adrenaline rush that kept them from feeling their cuts and injuries. Trust me, they felt them later.

Also, rumors spread that berserkers were werewolves or werebears (men who could turn into bears). Not true. They just acted like their spirit animals in order to scare enemies into paralysis. It often worked.

Berserkers styled themselves after the fierce, intense warriors they thought Odin wanted by his side at the great battle at the end of times. And if, in their craziness, they lost their lives—who cared? They'd spend their afterlife in Odin's hall in Asgard—Valhalla—partying, fighting, and feasting until they were needed for the final battle at Ragnarök.

Dying to fight and fighting to the death. It was the berserkers' way.

## ELVES AND SCARY GIANTS

Near Migard lay the lands of the dwarves and evil elves. We aren't going to tour those wild, uninhabited areas because such folk have absolutely no qualms about making humans suffer in countless painful and awful ways.

You may thank me for my generosity later with a feast. Plan accordingly—at least a couple of cows and pigs and barrels of mead for me. It takes a lot to fill my belly.

In the meantime, let's fly over to the land of the giants, *Jötunheim*. Don't worry. I will keep you safe. We're going to check out the spring of Mímir, the font of all knowledge and wisdom in our worlds.

You may want to consider a sip or two yourself, kid. I've seen your spelling tests.

# IT'S ALL FUN AND GAMES UNTIL ODIN LOSES AN EYE

As we fly over the mountains separating humans from giants, watch out for falling rocks and spiky chunks of ice. The rock-giants and the frost-giants—the forces of nature in all their chaotic glory—are in a constant battle for control. And they don't care who gets hurt in the process.

Whoa! Did you see that? Two ravens just zoomed past us. They are *Huginn* (Thought) and *Muninn* (Mind), Odin's ravens. My father was sometimes called "The Raven God" because of these two birds, as well as for the fact that ravens and other carrion birds often showed up to gnaw on the dead after a battle.

Every day, Huginn and Muninn fly around the Nordic realms and report all to Odin. When they aren't spying for him, they sit—one on each side—atop Odin's shoulders.

Ravens were common in our world, and they served to keep mortals in line. After all, if one flew by, you'd never know if it was "just" a regular raven or one of Odin's feathered spies ready to tattle-tell on you.

Odin sometimes worried about losing Huginn (Thought), but claimed he worried about Muninn (Mind) more. Yeah, Dad had no problem picking favorites. Anyway, he needn't have worried about either, especially after trading an eye for the wisdom of the world.

# AN EYE FOR A BRAIN, PLEASE

ntelligence and wisdom were so important to Odin, he was willing to trade a body part for it. Now that's commitment! Here's the story:

*Odin was sure he needed more wisdom and knowledge to prepare for the inevitable face-off with the bad guys. So, one day, he set off in his traveling hat and cloak, down the rainbow bridge and toward the land of the ice-giants.*

*In Jötunheim, the dominion of frost-giants, Odin made his way to a sacred well, guarded by an ancient wise giant named Mímir, whom we called "the rememberer."*

*"Oh, wise one," called Odin. "May I drink from your magic well? I seek greater wisdom for protecting all of our realms from the forces of destruction."*

*Mímir said, "With wisdom comes pain, for in these waters you will see every kind of sorrow and loss."*

*"I do not fear the pain of loss," Odin replied. "For along with it, wisdom also brings great beauty and joy."*

*"For such a gift," the ancient giant said, "I must have one of your eyes."*

*Odin did not even flinch. He plucked out his eye and handed it to the giant who placed it at the bottom of the well where even today it looks up into the faces of all who dare look down into it.*

*"Truly, you are a great king," Mímir said. "You may drink from the well of wisdom." He dipped a large horn*

*into the still water and handed it to Odin.*

*Odin drank deeply, and the waters of Mímir were truly miraculous, for even with only one eye, he could "see" and know twice what he had ever before.*

*"I am better prepared to protect us now," Odin said after he thanked the giant. He pulled his hat rakishly over the missing eye to hide his identity from those he passed and set off for Bifrost, the rainbow bridge connecting Middle Earth to his palace hall in Asgard.*

## THE EYEBALL IS WATCHING YOU

**F**inally, we're at Mímir's well. One word of advice: *don't* look down into it. Odin's giant eyeball staring back up at you will give you nightmares. I speak from experience. Not like I'm scared or anything. I mean, I *am* the god of strength and weather and mighty muscles. So one measly eyeball tracking me as I circle the well does not spook me or make me shudder *in the least.*

You can't scare *me*, eyeball!

Also, do not be alarmed by the pickled head over there resting on a stump. That's Mímir's noggin. In a fight between the gods, someone cut off his head in order to limit Odin's wisdom.

But my father saved the day by finding Mímir's head and sprinkling magic herbs over it, which kept it alive. You need only ask Mímir a question, and he will

answer it. However, the cost is watching that shriveled head open its dead eyes and speak through its wrinkled mouth. If you ask me, it isn't worth it, which is why I've never done it.

I mean, I'm smart enough as I am!

## BLOOD, BIRD POOP, AND THE BEGINNING OF GREAT POETRY

**L**ike our people, Odin valued poetry and good storytellers. My people especially loved "hero poetry," poems that praised the strength and honor of their warriors and leaders.

We called our poets *skalds*. The best skalds, we believed, received their talent from Odin himself. The story of how Odin obtained the gift of poetry to share with humans involves murder, beheadings, black-hearted dwarves, and bird poop. My favorite kind of story!

*After a long fight between the gods of nature (the Vanir) and the gods of Asgard (the Aesir), they drew up a truce that required each god to spit into a vat. From the great vat of slimy loogies, they fashioned a man named Kvasir.*

*Kvasir was the wisest human who ever lived. Even the gods respected his wisdom, for it had been fashioned from the essence of all of them. One day, two evil dwarves invited Kvasir to their home, where they killed him and brewed mead from his blood. Anyone* who drank this mead was magically turned into a poet or scholar. But the dwarves, not caring about such fine things, never drank it. Even so, being dwarves, they refused to share it.

Soon, the gods came looking for Kvasir.

"Oh, him?" one of the dwarves said. "He died choking on his own wisdom."

The gods suspected foul play, but they had no proof.

Meanwhile, the evil dwarves began a killing spree. First they drowned a giant, then murdered the giant's wife. The son of the murdered giants came after the dwarves. He grabbed them by the scruffs of their necks and headed out to sea to drown them.

They begged and pleaded for their lives. The giant's son agreed to spare them only under one condition— they give him the mead of poetry they'd brewed from Kvasir's blood.

"Done," they agreed.

The giant buried the jars of mead under a mountain and set his own daughter to guard the entrance. "Let no one enter," he advised. "Ever!"

Meanwhile, Odin had learned about the fate of Kvasir and was not happy about the murder, let alone that a giant had hoarded the magic mead made from Kvasir's blood. He traveled in disguise to the land of the giants and came to the farm of the brother of the giant who buried the mead.

Nine farmhands were busy mowing hay. Pulling

out a whetstone from his cloak, Odin called, "I can make your scythes sharper than a warrior's sword!"

They grew excited and allowed Odin to sharpen their equipment. When he was finished, they all remarked on the excellence of his work. "We want to buy your whetstone," they cried.

"Sure," Odin said. "But here's the price." He threw the stone into the air and as the nine lunged for it, they swung their scythes and cut each other's throats. Odin stepped over the bodies and spoke to the farm giant.

"Your farmhands killed each other," he announced. "But I can finish their jobs in exchange for your brother's magic mead."

"No guarantees, but if you bring in the crops, I'll speak to my brother on your behalf," the giant promised.

Odin worked hard and finished out the season. But when the two visited the giant who'd hidden the mead, his door was slammed in their faces.

"Let's just take the mead, if you know where it is," Odin said to the giant farmer. "Why should your brother hog all the treasure?"

So the two set off. At the mountain, Odin whipped out a hand drill and told the giant to bore a hole for him. Reluctantly, the giant complied and drilled all the way, not just through the mountain, but into the cave where the mead lay hidden.

Odin shifted his shape into a snake and wriggled his way through the hole. At this, the giant grew enraged, because he realized he'd been tricked by a god. He'd been tricked! And used. He went after the snake with his drill, but Odin was too quick and made it safely inside the mountain.

Finally, he emerged in the cave to face the giant's daughter, who guarded the vats of mead. Odin turned into his splendid, godly form.

"Are you one of the gods?" the giantess asked.

"I am, fair one," Odin said with a flirtatious smile.

The young giantess stood. "My father has abandoned me under this mountain, caring more for his treasures than for me," she said. "But you gods have not only come for me, but have also sent me a husband!"

Husband? Odin swallowed hard. "I . . . um, I cannot marry you," he said, "for I can stay only three days. But if you are all right with that, I will let all the gods know of your greatness and kindness, and you will be known as my temporary giant-wife."

The giantess agreed. On each of the three days he stayed with her, she allowed him to take a sip from one of the three vats of mead. But a single sip to Odin meant the entire vat! On the third day, he drained the last vat.

When it came time to say good-bye to the kind giantess, he kissed her and left the mountain. With all the mead still in his belly, he knew he had to return to Asgard quickly. He turned himself into a giant eagle and headed home.

The giantess's father, however, was watching the

mountain, and when he saw a great eagle fly out from the bottom of it, he knew a thief had stolen his mead. In a rage, he turned into a giant eagle himself and set off after Odin.

Now Odin had gotten a head start, but the giant in the form of an eagle flew strong and fast. He caught up just as Odin approached the walls protecting Asgard. The other gods quickly placed vats under the walls, and just as his eagle's head cleared it, Odin vomited all the mead into the waiting vats.

But the giant-as-eagle scared him so much that some of the mead had gone through his digestive system and emerged from his back end as bird poop, which fell just outside the walls. The giant-as-eagle screeched his rage when he saw Odin make it safely into Asgard.

From then on, the gods granted the mead made from Kvasir's blood to those mortals they thought worthy of their gift of poetry, especially the skalds who would tell stories of the great heroes. As for the mead droppings that fell outside the walls, they were for the occasional human fool to consume.

My people believed that great skalds had been Odin-chosen and that the Allfather had given them a sip of Kvasir's blood mead. That was true for some gifted poets. As for those who consumed what came out of Odin-as-eagle's back end? Their writing, like their breath, always stank. Literally.

# KILLER POETS =
# IDEAL VIKINGS

**M**y people loved Vikings who killed by day and wrote poetry by night—guys who were experts at drawing blood on the battlefield, then "killing" their audience at night with their wit. Mastering both violence and clever wordplay was every Viking's dream.

Few Vikings captured this ferocious combination better that Egil Skallagrímsson, who lived in the tenth century. Born in Iceland, Egil established his reputation as a wild and crazy guy at just three years old when his father refused to bring him to a feast. "You get too violent at these events," he told the child.

At seven, Egil murdered his first victim. He did not get in trouble for killing him; he got in trouble for hiding the body and not paying the family for the loss, which caused a great feud between the families.

When he was old enough, Egil joined a Viking crew. He spent most of the rest of his life raiding, killing, and pillaging to his heart's content. Egil once won a duel by throwing down his shield and sword, tackling his opponent, and tearing out the guy's windpipe with his teeth.

Along the way, he made an enemy of the powerful King of Norway, Erik Bloodaxe. Erik Bloodaxe eventually captured Egil, threw him in a dungeon, and called for his execution in the morning—by beheading. Egil spent all night writing a praise poem for ol' bloody-axe. Just as he was about to have his head chopped off, Egil requested to share his poem. King Erik reluctantly agreed.

So impressive was Egil's long rhyming poem, the king decided to spare his head. But only under one condition—if he promised never to cross King Erik's path again. Egil agreed, which only goes to prove how head-over-heels my people were for great poetry.

Still, despite my people's love for wordplay, sometimes they got a little lazy with words. For example, in Iceland and in other Scandinavian towns, my people called the political assembly of all free men a "Thing."

Seriously. T. H. I. N. G.

Not a congress of citizens. Not an assembly. Not even a town meeting. Just . . . a "Thing." At these Things, citizens elected chieftains and kings, voted on laws, and made legal judgments. There were no law books at these Things either. One man was charged with memorizing all the laws of the community. Guess what he was called? The "Law Speaker." And guess what they called the rocky outcrop where the Law Speaker recited all the laws? The "Law Rock." It gets better—Icelanders called the biggest government assembly they held the "Althing." It was during one of these Althings that Iceland officially turned its back on us Nordic gods and converted to Christianity.

My people may have written great poetry and sagas, but when it came to coming up with creative names in politics, I think they accidentally slurped the droppings Odin left outside Asgard's walls.

But enough of Midgard. Hop onto my goat-chariot and let's take a ride up the rainbow bridge to Asgard. It's time to meet the other gods.

# THE REALM
# OF THE GODS

**WAIT, YOU WON'T STEP** on our rainbow bridge because your science teacher says rainbows are nothing more than light refracting off water droplets?

*Oh, please!* Everyone knows rainbows are real and full of sparkling magic—especially our rainbow bridge, Bifrost. How else do you think we gods travel back and forth between Midgard and Asgard? And some people call *me* dumb. Honestly.

But, if you insist, you can stay on the chariot. I myself like to walk on Bifrost because, seriously, who wouldn't like to hop amongst the colors? My favorite rainbow color is red, because it reminds me of blood in battle. No . . . no, my favorite color is actually yellow, because it makes me think of mead. And with mead usually comes good food. It takes a lot of grub to keep my muscles impressively big, you know.

Anyway, that guy standing at the end of the bridge is Heimdall, the guardian. Be careful when you look at him—if he smiles at you, he'll blind you with his golden teeth.

Heimdall's job is to make sure no giants enter our realm. We hate giants, remember? It's a good thing you mortals are so tiny—he'll never mistake you for one of those enormous trolls, so you're safe from him trying to stomp you like a bug.

Blowing that ginormous horn he holds in his hand is how Heimdall will signal Ragnarök, the end of times. Hopefully, he won't be using it anytime soon.

As Heimdall allows us through, you will see that we've entered a land of wild forests and endless green growth. We've landed in *Vanaheim*, home of the *Vanir*, gods of nature and fertility. They live up here with us *Aesir* gods in their own section of Asgard. We once fought against the Vanir and made peace by spitting into a vat together and creating Kvasir (remember him?).

Look, here come two of the most famous gods of the Vanir—Frey and his sister Freya. As the gods of fertility and growth, Frey and Freya emanate warm sunlight and the smell of green earth.

Two cats pull Freya's chariot. Cats! These are no

ordinary house kitties, either. They are the strong, sleek, wild cats native to Scandinavia. Freya is also the goddess of both love and war. Love poetry was often dedicated to her.

As for the war part, Freya took half the fallen on the battlefield, while the Valkyries—she-warriors on horses—took the other half to Odin. Everyone knows Odin keeps those warriors in fighting shape for Ragnarök, but no one knows what Freya does with them. And everybody is either too wowed by her beauty or too scared of her power to ask!

Meanwhile, a golden pig pulls her brother Frey's chariot. The same dwarves that made my hammer made his porcine puller. Frey is in charge of the dwarves and elves—which must be the reason why they *also* gave him the ship that folds into his pocket *and* the magic sword that fights on its own, which really makes no sense to me. I mean, I don't want to sound greedy, but I think I should've gotten that sword. I'm the one who's big and strong and can actually destroy giants.

Frey? He's so foolish he fell in *love* with a giantess. Who does that? They're our natural enemies! And *then* Frey got tricked out of his magic sword by his own servant while wooing his humongous "beloved." What. A. Waste.

And guess who's destined to be killed by a giant during Ragnarök? Yup. Frey. His foolishness is making me angry and you know what that means—

thunder and lightning and all manner of weatherly misery. So let's get away from him and head on over to Asgard proper.

## BEWARE THE BIG BAD WOLF

As we are still in the wilds outside the walls of Asgard, you may be aware of strange noises. Do not be alarmed. That growling and snapping you hear is *Fenrir*, the monstrous wolf destined to destroy Odin during Ragnarök. Let's go say hi.

Come on. Don't be scared. He is tied up and can't attack us, despite his meanness. Oh, and remember who the father is?

That's right—*Loki!*

Loki, if you recall, had three children with a giantess, all of them monsters. There's Jörmungandr, the serpent in the sea; Hel in the underworld; and Fenrir, the big bad wolf. Fenrir, it was prophesied, would devour Odin during Ragnarök. Chaining this beast-o'-death was no easy challenge:

*As Fenrir grew and grew, we gods became concerned. Some wanted to kill the beast, but everyone agreed we couldn't do such a thing within Asgard. Unleashing him on the other realms was unthinkable. So the decision was made to tie him up.*

*But when we chained him, the wolf gave us an evil grin, fluffed his coat, steeled his muscles, and the*

rings broke apart like paper. Suitably alarmed, we gods tried again.

This time, we returned with a chain of immense size and strength. Each iron link was the size of a ship's anchor. With great effort, we wound the chains around Fenrir. The wolf strained a little harder this time, leaving him panting, but again, he shattered the chain.

We had grown very concerned by this time. Together, we decided that only the dwarves could make a chain strong enough to hold the wolf. The dwarves leaped at the challenge—but only after negotiating for a giant payment of gold.

The dwarves finally presented us with a fetter that looked like a silk ribbon. "You have got to be kidding us!" Odin cried. "That will never hold the wolf!"

It would, claimed the dwarves, because it was made of magic.

"Magic what?" I asked.

"It's made of six things," the dwarves explained. "Cat footsteps, mountain roots, the beard of a woman, bird spit, bear sinews, and the breath of a fish."

That seemed reasonable. So we went back to the woods to snare Fenrir. As for the wolf, he laughed when he saw the ribbon. "You insult me if you think that will hold me!" he cried. "I will not be bound by a ribbon."

Still, the wolf's pride was pricked. He couldn't show cowardice, but he suspected a trick. "Fine," he finally said. "But I will allow it only if one of you gods puts a

*hand in my mouth."*

*None of us wanted to take the risk (hey, I needed both hands to fight the giants!), but finally, brave Tyr, the god of war and glory, stepped up. He put his hand in the wolf's smelly mouth, and the others quickly wound the ribbon around and around the wolf until none was left.*

*Fenrir struggled against his new fetters, but the more he moved, the tighter they got. He'd been tricked! He snapped his jaws and Tyr lost his hand. We deemed the loss worth it.*

*Tyr was not so sure.*

*Still, we were all safe from the beast. At least until Ragnarök.*

You don't want to come up and pet Fenrir? You sure? Then let's head on over to the realm of us gods.

## WALLS THAT SEPARATE THE GODS FROM THE POOP OF MEDIOCRITY

**A**h, the strong walls of Asgard emerge from the mist. Aren't they magnificent? By the way, watch your step. We'll soon be entering the area where Odin-as-eagle squirted the droppings of bad poetry as he flew over the wall.

You wouldn't want to step in it and then spend the rest of your life wondering if your writing has the whiff of waste. Just sayin'.

Anyway, the walls of Asgard are impressive, are they not? They soar into the sky and are almost as thick as my biceps. We need them this big and strong to keep out nasty giants. And yet we got a giant to build them for us—for free! Here's how we tricked him:

*The walls around Asgard had fallen during the war with the Vanir gods, which left Asgard vulnerable to evil giants. Every day, the gods looked at the rubble and said, "We need to fix that!" But no god wanted to actually do the work.*

*One day, Heimdall the guardian allowed a builder and his horse to pass up the rainbow bridge because the man promised to build us a wall. "My wall will protect you from frost-giants, rock-giants, and all manner of evil," the workman told Odin and the rest of us.*

*"How long will it take you?" Odin asked.*

*"Three seasons," the man said. "But my price is steep."*

*"What is it?" Allfather asked.*

*"The hand of the goddess Freya in marriage!"*

*At this, Freya gasped and stood. As the goddess of fertility, she was the most revered goddess of all. How dare this man try to claim her! But before she could berate him, the builder added, "But that's not all. I must also have the sun and the moon as well."*

*All of us gods cried out in anger then. Impossible!*

*Outrageous! Tell him to get lost!*

The sly god Loki, however, suggested a plan. Gathering us in private, he said, "We can get what we want without having to give him anything. Trust me on this." Not everyone trusted Loki, but everyone wanted the wall, so we reluctantly agreed.

Loki went back to the man and said, "You have a deal, but only if you complete the job in one season instead of three, and only if you have no one help you except your horse."

The builder thought this was a bit extreme—he'd have to work fast—but knowing that he'd get Freya as well as the sun and the moon convinced him. He agreed.

The man was an expert wall-maker and he worked very fast. His strong horse tirelessly pulled enormous stones and boulders to the site. Three days before the deadline, we gods began to panic. It looked like the builder might finish the wall after all! Then we would lose the lovely Freya and plunge the world into darkness without the sun and moon.

Odin called upon Loki and raged at him. "You're the one who came up with this deal. You have to fix it!"

"But I didn't think he could actually build the wall in such a short amount of time," Loki whined.

We did not care. "Keep the builder from finishing the wall by the deadline, or you will lose your life," Odin warned.

Loki was sufficiently motivated to come up with a plan.

*Later, when the man led his stallion into the woods in search of stones to finish off the gate, Loki turned himself into a mare, a female horse. The mare whinnied at the builder's horse as he passed. The stallion's ears pricked and he huffed to show his interest. The mare pranced out in front of the stallion and then sprinted away. The stallion quickly followed, despite the man roaring at him to stop. The stallion and the mare disappeared for days. The builder could not finish the wall. He'd lost the bet. He got so mad, he popped into his true form—a giant!*

*I, Thor, took my magic hammer and shattered the giant into millions of tiny shards. After all, he'd tricked us!*

*As for Loki, he stayed away for a long time. No one complained. Finally, he returned to Asgard—after the rest of us gods had finished the gate, of course—bearing a gift for Odin. It was a gray horse with eight legs. Loki, as the mare, had given birth to the creature. That's right, Loki had a baby!*

*Odin named the eight-legged creature Sleipnir and prized it for its speed in traveling between the worlds.*

Despite our hatred of Loki, even Odin couldn't look a gift horse in the mouth. Luckily, Sleipnir was the only "child" of Loki that didn't turn into an evil monster.

# BEWARE OLD LADIES
## WITH SCISSORS

ow that we are inside the walls, we'll head on over to the clearing near the Well of Urd. That's where we gods like to gossip—er, I mean, hold our daily meetings. So straighten up and look sharp as we approach, please.

Oh look, there are the three Norns—the goddesses of fate. *Bow to them, quick!* You never want them mad at you. Their names are "What Has Been," "What Is," and "What Must Be." They spin the threads of life for all creatures, including us gods. When it's your time to go, they'll snip your thread and you'll fall to the ground like a broken marionette.

If you're a Viking, you'd better hope they snip it when you're in the middle of a battle. Otherwise, to boring Hel you go!

Wait, you say the story of three goddesses who weave the fates of all sounds vaguely familiar? That the ancient Greeks had similar goddesses they called "The Fates"? Please. We Vikings came first. No? The ancient Greeks lived more than a thousand years *before* us?

Oh. Then like good Vikings, we may have plundered their concept and made it our own. It's the Viking way, after all.

# ODIN'S ULTIMATE SACRIFICE

O din paid a steep price to gain even more wisdom. Remember how he gave up his eye to drink from Mímir's spring of knowledge? And how that eyeball—which doesn't give me the creeps *at all*—still sits at the bottom of the well staring up at us?

Well, he went even further to obtain the wisdom of the runes, the written language of our people. Now, your little *dirt-diggers* (what my Egyptian godfriend Anubis calls your archaeologists) say that runes emerged as a combination of old Germanic, Mediterranean letters, and even ancient petroglyphs.

What foolishness! How would that even happen? And they call *me* "a little thick."

We Vikings know the truth—Odin hung himself on the tree of life over the Well of Urd in our lowest realms to earn the wisdom of our written word. Here's the story:

*Odin yearned for all knowledge and wisdom. When he saw that the three Norns read the sacred language of runes from the Well of Urd, he determined to learn their secrets. But Odin knew wisdom couldn't be forced—it had to be earned.*

*So, he made of himself the ultimate sacrifice. He speared himself in the side and then hung himself from the great ash tree of life, Yggdrasill. He hung there— between life and death, lightness and darkness—for nine days and nine nights, staring down into the waters of Urd until the wisdom of the runes was finally revealed to him.*

*And with the runes came the charms for healing, securing victory in battle, calming the seas, putting out fires, and many more good works. Odin then shared that sacred knowledge with his wisest followers.*

Odin put a whole new spin on the idea of "dying to learn something." It's a good thing he did, though, because our runes are very important to us.

Runes told fortunes, provided protection, and cast spells. My people left runes all over the place. They were used for everything from making claim to the ordinary—"I own this box"—to sharing the mythic tales of bloodthirsty warrior kings.

Want to try your hand at reading runes? Use the chart below to translate this wise truth:

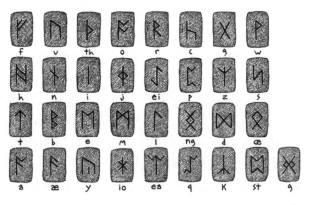

# ROTTEN RUNE QUACKS

Runic writing has been found on everything from giant stones to tiny wood slivers. The words have been carved on seal tusks, whale bones, metal jewelry, and war weapons. Learned men and women who used runes for magical purposes were considered very powerful. But bad runic writers could cause more damage than good.

Once, a woman went to a rune reader for help, but he wrote the wrong charm, and the woman became deathly ill. A rune expert discovered the error, carved the correct rune on a whale bone, hung it over the woman's bed, and—*poof!*—she was instantly healed. Guess who that rune master was? The man who saved the woman's life was none other than that silver-tongued Viking skald, Egil Skallagrímsson, who saved his head with poetry.

In another story, a rune master carved protective runes on his drinking horn. When an enemy tried to poison him, the runes caused the horn to break in two. Now that's what I call using your horn!

# MEETING OF THE GODS

As we approach the Well of Urd, you'll notice it's kind of crowded. We've hit it during the daily gossip—I mean, discussion—session. Ah, there is Odin himself. A word of advice—do not stare into our Allfather's empty eye socket. He doesn't like it. Also, do not try to scare the pet ravens on his shoulders—Huginn and Muninn. If they squawk in his ears and irritate him, he may set them to peck out your eyes, which he would do because you're clearly not a warrior and Odin prefers warriors.

Oh, please. Don't act all insulted. You're *not* a warrior, no matter how many times you play one on your game box. Just nod respectfully, and Odin won't smite you for it. Be sure also to say hello to Frigg, Odin's wife, goddess of marriage and motherhood.

Nordic women, like our goddesses, were strong and tough and had no problem dealing with a pup like you. Our women could own property and often managed the homestead—including large farms—while hubby was out a-plundering. Some even liked to fight and joined their men in their raids. These tough fighters were known as shield maidens. That's right—equal opportunity pillaging!

Mímir's bodiless head is over there on the lip of the Well of Urd. Remember him? He was beheaded during the war between the gods. Odin preserved the head with herbs and consults it on a regular basis. Mímir was the wisest of the wise and still shares his wisdom, but only with Odin.

That's why you'll occasionally see Odin bring that pickled and herbed head to his ear. It's pretty unsettling to have both heads—Odin's and Mímir's—turn your way, scowling, while they whisper together. If that happens to you, *run*. I tell you this from experience.

## HOW LOKI UPSET THE APPLECART

**S**ee that young goddess over there? That's Idunn, the goddess of youth and beauty. She's carrying a basket of golden apples that we gods eat regularly to stay young, strong, and fit. Without them, we would age fast, becoming brittle and old.

Idunn is the sweetest and kindest goddess in our realm. Nobody would ever think of messing with her, right? Wrong. Only one person would dare, and you already know who it is. This is the story:

*One day, Odin, Loki, and a friend went exploring in Midgard. After many, many hours, they grew hungry. When they came across a herd of oxen, they slaughtered one and began to cook it over a fire.*

*Their mouths watered, and their stomachs grumbled. After plenty of roasting time, they pulled their dinner out, but it was as red and raw as the moment they slaughtered it.*

*"What's this?" Odin cried. "We must have miscalculated the roasting time because we're so hungry." He shoved the meat back on the fire. This time they gave it an even longer cooking time, but again, the meat came out completely uncoated.*

Loki stomped his foot. "This is ridiculous!" he cried. "Something weird is at work here."

"That's right," said an eagle above them. "And it's me. I will allow the meat to be cooked if you let me have the choicest bits."

The gods weren't happy about this, but they agreed. The eagle flew down and took the best parts of the ox in his talons and began to devour the meat. Loki, outraged at the bird's greediness, took a staff and tried to beat the bird with it, but the staff magically stuck to the bird's body instead.

When the eagle took off in flight, Loki could not let go because of the magic, so he hung on for dear life. The furious eagle battered Loki against trees, rocks, and cliffs. Loki begged to be released. The eagle (a giant in disguise), said he would free him only under one condition: that Loki would bring him the goddess Idunn and her golden apples. Desperate, Loki agreed, and the eagle let him go.

Loki went to sweet and naïve Idunn and said, "Guess what? I found the most wonderful golden fruit in the woods—possibly even better than yours! Do you want to see?"

Curious, Idunn nodded. "Bring your basket of apples," Loki said, "so you can compare the golden fruits."

When they walked outside the gates of Asgard, the giant in his eagle form snatched the goddess and her apples and flew away to his ice mountain. Soon after, the gods began to age quickly. Their skin wrinkled, their hair turned gray, and their muscles weakened. Nobody could find Idunn and her apples anywhere.

At the council by the Well of Urd, the gods wondered who had last seen the goddess. Of course, it was Loki, and they shook the story out of him.

"But the eagle-giant was going to kill me! I had to promise," the little weasel explained. He did not want to try to get her back.

"You must," Odin warned. "Or I will torture and kill you."

Loki agreed. Freya loaned him her falcon skin, and he flew over to where the giant had hidden Idunn. He muttered runes that turned her and her apples into a nut he could carry in his talons, and he set off for Asgard.

The giant soon discovered her missing, turned into an eagle again, and set after her. The eagle was faster than the falcon and nearly caught up just as Loki was approaching the walls of Asgard. Odin ordered all the kindling wood from all the palaces placed right outside the walls. Loki, as an agile falcon, made it past the walls, but Odin had the fires lit just as the eagle approached. The creature burst into flame and fell into a heap inside Asgard. We gods then finished him off.

As for Loki, after putting down his prize, he crossed his arms and laughed at the bald heads and bent backs of the gods (he didn't look so great himself, but that never stopped him). But one look from Odin and Loki got to *work. Uttering the magic runes, he turned Idunn and her apples back into their regular forms. Idunn, glad to be home, moved among the gods, offering her golden apples of youth.*

Loki, once again, proved to be the rotten apple that (almost) spoiled our barrel of golden good looks. For that, I'll never forgive him. I mean, I lost muscle mass! Especially in my extraordinary biceps! I still have nightmares about that horror.

## DETAILS, DETAILS

**D**id you know that almost all of the days of the week are named after my fellow Nordic gods? Check it out:

**Sunday:** for Sol, goddess of the sun, Sun's day
**Monday:** for Mani, goddess of the moon, Mani's day
**Tuesday:** for Tyr, god of war, Tyr's day
**Wednesday:** for Odin, sometimes known as Woden
**Thursday:** for me, Thor!
**Friday:** for Frigg, goddess of marriage, Frigg's day

Saturday did not come from us, but from the Romans— Saturn's day. But hey, you can't have everything, right?

Beyond the days of the week, you moderns took lots of other Nordic words from us. You can thank us for *berserk, crook, dregs, hit, oaf, outlaw, ransack, rotten,*

94

*scare, skull, slaughter, sly,* and *troll.* And don't think I haven't noticed that all these words are often used to describe us Vikings.

I couldn't be any prouder!

And, like any Viking worth his sardines, you continued plundering words, taking for yourselves some of my favorites, including *cake, egg, reindeer, steak,* and *wings.* Which reminds me, I'm hungry. *Mmmmm,* I could eat a whole goat right now. And maybe an ox, too. With a side of reindeer stew and fried walrus tongues.

Oh, sorry. That was not an earthquake. Just my tummy growling.

I've always had a big appetite, you know. And once it almost cost me my magic hammer, Mjöllnir. Here's what happened:

*The giant king had stolen Mjöllnir. We had to get it back because my hammer and me were the only things standing between the giants and total destruction!*

*Loki borrowed Freya's falcon skin and flew over the giant's lair demanding the hammer back. The giant would part with it only under one condition—if the goddess Freya would marry him. Loki flew back and told the council.*

*Freya, of course, adamantly refused.*

*"Why don't you, Thor, pretend to be Freya?" suggested Heimdall the Watcher. "We could dress you up*

*as a bride, and you could snatch the hammer back once you're inside the hall."*

[For the record, I did *not* like this plan at all. Everybody else loved it, though, so I was overruled. I have to say, too, that everybody took *way* too much pleasure in dressing me up in frilly things. Way too much.]

*They stuffed me into a wedding gown, pinned me with jewels, and stuck a veil over my head. Loki and I headed to the giant's hall for the so-called wedding. At the feast, the smell of the food really got to me. I figured I might as well enjoy myself, so I scarfed one roasted oxen and eight salmon, wiping my greasy hands on my wedding dress, while I sent bones flying out from under my veil. I topped it off with multiple large horns of mead and belched so loudly the shields on the walls rattled. The giant looked at me warily. "Wow, she really eats a lot," he said. "And, um . . . her manners are atrocious!"*

*"Oh, it's just because she hasn't eaten in days before coming here," Loki said, surreptitiously elbowing me to get a grip on my appetite. "She was too excited to eat!"*

*The giant accepted this, even though I had eaten just before leaving Asgard. (What can I say? It takes a lot to keep my strength up.)*

*Nevertheless, I didn't like how that giant was staring at me, so my eyes turned red-hot like they do before I send an electrical storm.*

*Alarmed, the giant cried, "And her eyes are so red! Why are her eyes so red?"*

*"It's only because she was so happy about marrying you, she couldn't sleep for a week," Loki explained.*

*Seeing that my temper was nearing the boiling point, Loki jumped up and said, "Bring the hammer and let us hold the ceremony right now!"*

*The moment I saw Mjöllnir, I jumped up, snatched it from my intended's hands, and destroyed every giant in the room. I had gotten my hammer back, killed some giants, and eaten an excellent meal to boot.*

All in all, aside from my having to wear a veil and a wedding dress, it turned out to be a very good day. I haven't been separated from Mjöllnir since.

# DESTINATION PARTY PALACE, A.K.A. VALHALLA

**ODIN'S HALL, OTHERWISE KNOWN AS** the "Hall of Slain Warriors," is the most famous of all the halls in Valhalla. Now, some of your modern Nordic scholars question whether Valhalla is actually up here in Asgard or down below next door to Hel's lovely place. All the dead warriors confuse them, it seems. But then again, your scholars aren't warriors, so how can they be expected to know up from down?

Anyway, Valhalla is like an endless zombie slumber party: Everyone's dead. They spend all night re-killing each other. Then they wake up in the morning ready to do it all again. Only no brains are consumed. Just pig.

In Valhalla, we feast on the flesh of a giant boar

(a wild pig) that gets slaughtered every night and, like our men, magically regenerates in the morning. Zombie warriors feasting on an endless supply of zombie bacon. Now that's my kind of party!

True, from the outside, Odin's hall doesn't much look like a "palace"—it looks like a gigantic version of the kind of longhouse my people lived in during the Middle Ages, including a thatched roof. But its size—as well as the giant wolf guarding the entrance and the immense eagle hovering over the roof—lets you know it's something special.

Oh, and don't worry, the wolf won't hurt us—it's not Fenrir, after all.

Now, pick an entrance. Any entrance. There are 540 of them from which to choose. And each one is so wide, eight hundred warriors can line up—shoulder-to-shoulder—when it's time to march out and meet the enemy during the final battle against evil at Ragnarök.

As we step inside, let me give you a word of advice— do not engage these warriors. They're always looking for a fight, and you, kid, wouldn't last three seconds.

## GOLDEN SHIELDS AND WALLS OF SPEARS

Truly, this place is a warrior's dream: endless golden shields hang from the roof, while the rafters are made of spear shafts. The floor is packed dirt, but you can't see it, what with the blood and gore we constantly track inside from our bouts in the fighting fields. And yeah, that was an arm we just saw flying by. *Duck!* There goes a head. *Oh hey, nice to see you again, too, Sigurd!*

Sometimes, our warriors bring back body parts from the field before their friends heal up and regenerate, just for laughs. But don't worry. It's all just fun and games to us!

How did all these warriors get here? Look up. See those young women on horses flying through the air with dead warriors in their arms? They're Valkyries. And they are about to drop another dead-but-soon-to-be-alive-again warrior on us. Literally.

Again, *duck.*

## VALKYRIES, JUDGES ON THE FLY

**V**alkyries are the "Choosers of the Slain." Dressed in armor and helmets and riding magic flying horses, they fly-ride around the battlefield looking for slain warriors brave enough to help Odin during Ragnarök. They take only half the dead. Freya takes the other half. What she does with them, we don't know. And we don't ask.

The Valkyries work for Odin. They sometimes called swan maidens because one saga claims they wore clothing made of swan feathers. When they weren't collecting the dead and dropping them off here, they feasted with the warriors.

Let me point out some of the more famous Vikings they've "dropped off" in Valhalla:

**Erik Bloodaxe:** He's the guy over there swinging—you guessed it—a bloody axe, his weapon of choice. He was king of Northumbria (a region in northern England and parts of Scotland) and king of Norway for a time, too. Erik was a fierce warrior and ruler. Legend has it he died battling five other kings in an epic kill-off. If he comes anywhere near you, tell him you're not a king so he won't challenge you to step outside and cut you in two.

**Harald Hardradi:** Hardradi means "hard ruler," and Harald earned his reputation by being ruthless and vicious. He invaded regions in Russia and was a military commander in Constantinople. Eventually, he became king of Norway and raided Denmark. He invaded England, wanting to be king there, too, but lost his life in a key battle. Harad's the one in the corner over there grabbing everything around him and yelling, "Mine! Mine! Mine!"

**Gunnar Hamundarson:** Gunnar, an Icelandic hero-warrior, was so strong he could jump the height of a man, even when wearing full armor. He could also throw stones from a mile away and hit his target between the eyes. And he was a great archer and blade-fighter. Gunnar's the guy at the table taking bets on whether he can jump high enough to pull the tail of one of the Valkyries' horses flying above us.

See that empty bench at the feasting table? That's for Olaf Tryggvason, a great Viking and former king of Norway. The reason he is not here is because he became Christian, so he went somewhere else after his death. However, we remember him because he was a super-vicious guy who killed many people in his attempt to convert the masses to his new religion. Plus, he died in battle against other Vikings, so we figured he at least deserved a seat.

The hall is packed with countless other warriors, as you can see, including Canute the Great, Sweyn Forkbeard, and others. The heroes of legend are here, too, including Sigmund—who pulled from a tree a magic sword Odin had buried to the hilt. No one else was able to pull it out except for Sigmund, a story much like King Arthur's "sword in the stone."

Next to Sigmund is Sigurd, a brave hero who defeated a dragon, as well as the brilliant shield maiden Brynhild, who taught him the magic of the runes. Also nearby is Hogni, who was so tough he laughed in the face of the assassin who cut his heart from his chest.

Really, the list of heroes and warriors in Valhalla is endless, and I just got a whiff of roasting pig. I'm suddenly *starving*. So, uhm . . . get out of my way, kid.

Wait, you want me to escort you home? But . . . but there's magic *bacon* here! Look, just head out on your own through one of Valhalla's 540 doors, make a left at Fenrir, and go down the rainbow bridge. Easy peasy.

What? You're scared to go by yourself? Please. Have we Vikings taught you *nothing*? You must fearlessly face your fate. No, seriously. I'm not leaving a feast to guide you out. I've got my priorities, you know.

Wait, you say there are rumors of giants—*giants*, my eternal enemies—walking around up here? Well, as the god of protection, I *must* escort you out.

You're not tricking me, are you, kid?

# THE END OF TIMES

As we pass Fenrir, I'm not surprised we don't see any giants yet. The only good thing about this "bad dog" wolf is that he would create a ruckus if giants came near. They smell, you know.

All of Loki's children, by the way, including Fenrir, are much like him—tricky, sneaky, and bent on destruction. In fact, it is thanks to Loki and his spawn that all of these wonderful Nordic realms will be destroyed.

We call it the "end of times," or Ragnarök.

Ragnarök means "Doom of the Gods," or the time when Loki's children—Fenrir, Jörmungandr, and Hel—will defeat us. Yup. Me, Odin, and nearly all the gods will be killed in a final battle.

Ragnarök promises to be an incredible bloodbath. Fenrir will break his bonds and devour Odin. Jörmungandr, the giant serpent, will rear up against me. I will defeat him, but the serpent's venomous breath will ultimately take me down, too.

What happens to Loki? After my brother Heimdall sounds the alarm signaling the war has begun, that sneaky son-of-a-giant attacks Heimdall. They end up killing each other.

Meanwhile, all of the dead warriors in Valhalla will rise up to help us fight, but it won't matter. When the giants, led by Loki's daughter Hel, arrive in their ship made from the fingernails and toenails of the dead, it will soon be all over.

Wait, let me repeat that: The giants will arrive on a boat made of *the crusty, snaggled, yellow fingernails and toenails of the dead.* Only one of Loki's kids could've come up with that level of grossness.

Even so, my people took heart in the fact that although we old gods will die, the world will not actually be destroyed. A single man and woman will survive. Some sources say Baldur and his blind brother Hod will come back, as will some of Odin's kids. My own sons will inherit my hammer!

And then the whole cycle of creation and destruction will begin again.

There's Bifrost, the rainbow bridge. Hey, I know a

super-fast way for you to get home. All you have to do is sit right down on the edge of our rainbow.

Go ahead. *Sit.* Comfy? Good. Now I just take several steps back and then give you—a running SHOVE!

*Woohoo!*

World's best slide, am I riiiiiight?

That's what you get for tricking me into escorting you to Bifrost. But you've got to admit, even my punishments are fun. See why everyone loved me?

Well, it's time for me to return to the feast in Valhalla. These muscles aren't going to get any bigger or stronger without another round of mead and magic barbecued pig, you know.

Say hello to the elves in Midgard for me!

See ya next time, kid!

# THOR'S GUIDE TO NORSE GODS AND MONSTERS

**Aesir:** My family of gods, led by Odin, who live within the vast walls of Asgard.

**Baldur:** Baldur was the god of beauty, wisdom, and general goodness. Then Loki had to go and ruin it all by finding the one thing that could harm him—mistletoe—and using it to kill him.

**Dwarves:** They began as maggots crawling around the dead body of Ymir, the frost-giant who started it all, until Odin turned them into mini-men with exceptional forge-crafting skills. The grouchy little folk prefer to live underground.

**Fenrir:** One of Loki's children, he's a monstrous wolf-beast fated to kill Odin during Ragnarök. The ultimate "bad dog."

**Frey:** One of the Vanir gods, Frey is associated with nature and growing things. He is a powerful god who made use of a golden pig to drive his chariot, a boat that he could fold to fit into his pocket, and a magical sword that got stolen (which I, Thor, would never have allowed to happen—just sayin').

**Freya:** Goddess of beauty and strength, she rides into battle on a chariot drawn by cats (if you've ever tried to control a cat, then you know just how powerful she is!). She is also Vanir, and takes half the dead from the battlefield, while the Valkyries take the other half for Odin.

**Frigg:** Odin's wife, Frigg is powerful and beautiful. She is also the mother of Baldur and has the gift of prophecy. However, she usually keeps quiet about what she foresees.

**Giants:** Terrible gigantic creatures that come in the forms of ice, rock, wolves, and other creatures. They hate us gods and wait for the day to attack us. It is my job to keep them away from Asgard.

**Heimdall:** Guardian of the rainbow bridge, Bifrost, Heimdall has golden teeth and always walks around with a giant horn he uses to warn us of impending doom.

**Hel:** Loki's daughter, she presides over the land of the dead in Niflheim. Hel is loads of fun (not). Her bed is called "Sick bed," her plate is known as "Hunger," and her knife is named "Famine." She's not the life of the party, but the death of it.

**Huginn:** One of Odin's two pet ravens, Huginn is known as "Thought." Odin cares less about him than he does about Muninn, the raven of "Memory" or "Mind." Because that's just how he rolls.

**Hymir:** A giant who took me fishing and panicked when I caught Jörmungandr, the serpent who surrounds the earth, and cut my line.

**Idunn:** Sweet-faced, good-natured goddess who protects the apples of youth for us gods in Asgard.

**Jörmungandr:** Another one of Loki's horrible kids, he is the terrible Midgard Serpent that I will defeat during Ragnarök. In his death throes, Jörmungandr will breathe his venomous breath all over me and kill me in return (the beast).

**Kvasir:** The original spit-man, he was made from the combined saliva of the Aesir and Vanir gods during a peace treaty. Although extremely wise, he wasn't wise enough to avoid being killed by a couple of greedy dwarves who mixed his blood with honey to make the Mead of Poetry.

**Loki:** Blood-brother to Odin, Loki is a trickster, a shape-shifting, mischievous god who spawned terrible monster children and will ultimately usher in the destruction of the world as we know it. Nobody can figure out exactly what hold he has over Odin in order to stay part of the Aesir family of gods.

**Mímir:** A wise guy beheaded by the Vanir during the war with the Aesir gods. Odin preserved his head with magic spells and herbs and regularly consults with the dead-head, who whispers words of wisdom into Odin's ear.

**Muninn:** One of Odin's ravens, Muninn represents "Memory" or "Mind." Odin has a soft spot for this raven and worries about losing him.

**Nidhogg:** The serpent who gnaws at the roots of the tree of life, Yggdrasill. When he gets bored of that, he chews on the corpses down by Hel's place.

**Norns:** Three goddesses (and/or giantesses) of fate and destiny. One snip of your life-thread and you're done.

**Odin:** My dad and the top god of all the gods, also known as the god of poetry, war, battle, and death.

**Sindri:** The dwarf who forged Thor's hammer, as well as Odin's magically reproducing rings and Frey's golden boar.

**Thor:** Yours truly, I was everyone's favorite god because I protected both Asgard and Midgard (where you little people live) against the giants with my trusty magical hammer, Mjöllnir. I am also often called god of thunder, but my main job was protection.

**Tyr:** The god of war. Also brave enough to stick his hand in the mouth of wolf-beast Fenrir, who promptly bit it off.

**Valkyries:** Beautiful young women dressed in battle gear who ride flying horses over the combat zones. They select the bravest warriors who die in battle and bring them back to Valhalla, where they will help Odin and the rest of us gods fight during Ragnarök.

**Vanir:** Fertility and nature gods who live outside the walls of Asgard. We Aesir gods once fought them, but eventually we became friends and allies. They will help us fight the bad guys during Ragnarök.

# GLOSSARY

**Aesir:** One of the two tribes of Nordic gods, the other being the Vanir. Odin and his family of gods, including Thor, are Aesir gods.

**Allfather:** Title often used to refer to Odin, the most powerful of the Norse gods.

**Asgard:** One of the nine realms in Norse mythology; where the Aesir gods live.

**Bifrost:** Rainbow bridge connecting Asgard to Midgard or Middle Earth.

**Fjord:** A long, narrow inlet or body of water, often surrounded by steep cliffs.

**Hel:** Daughter of Loki, Hel presides over the land of the dead; her name is often used to refer to the place over which she rules.

**Járngreiper:** "Iron grasper," the gloves Thor uses to catch his hammer.

**Megingjardar:** Thor's magic belt; it doubles his already impressive power and strength.

**Midgard:** Also known as Middle Earth, where humans reside alongside dwarves and giants.

**Mjöllnir:** Thor's magic hammer, which has the destructive power of lightning and can smash mountains.

**Niflheim:** Sometimes referred to as the "mist-world," it is often associated with the underworld, because it's under the Tree of Life. Hel presides there.

**Ragnarök:** The "Doom of the Gods," when the gods will

battle the forces of evil and darkness and lose. During Ragnarök, the world will sink into nothingness, only to be reborn and begin the cycle of birth and destruction again.

**Runes:** Letters in a set of alphabets used by Norse people that came from Mediterranean languages as well as Germanic symbols. Rune writing was used for communication and in magic ritual.

**Valhalla:** Odin's majestic hall in Asgard where war heroes go after falling in battle; there, they feast and fight in preparation to fight alongside Odin during Ragnarök.

**Vanir:** One of two groups of gods in Norse mythology (the other being the Aesir). The Vanir are associated with nature, fertility, and magic. They live in the wilds outside the walls encircling the Aesir gods.

**Vikings:** Term used to describe seafaring attackers in longships coming from the North or Scandinavia.

**Viking Age:** The era of vast expansion in Europe by Scandinavian warriors during the eighth through the eleventh centuries CE (Common Era). The Viking Age ended when Christianity was adopted throughout the region.

**Yggdrasill:** The mythological great ash Tree of Life that connects all of the Norse realms.

# BIBLIOGRAPHY

## PRIMARY SOURCES

Ahmad Ibn Fadhlan, *Account of His Travels to the King of the Volga Bulgars For the Caliph of Baghdad.*

Snorri Sturluson, *Heimskringla.*

Snorri Sturluson, *Poetic Edda.*

Snorri Sturluson, *Prose Edda.*

Authors Unknown, *Sagas of the Icelanders.*

## SECONDARY SOURCES

Brown, Nancy Marie. *Song of the Vikings.* New York: Macmillan, 2012.

Colum, Padraic. *Nordic Gods and Heroes.* New York: Dover, 1996.

Crossley-Holland, Kevin. *The Norse Myths.* New York: Pantheon Books, 1980.

D'aulaire, Ingri and Edgar. *D'aulaires' Book of Norse Myths.* New York: New York Review of Books, 1967.

Ellis, Hilda Roderick. *The Road to Hel: A Study of the Conception of the Dead in Old Norse Literature.* Cambridge: Cambridge University Press, 2013 (first edition 1943).

Green, Roger Lancelyn. *Myths of the Norsemen.* New York: Puffin Classics, 1970.

Hall, Richard. *The World of the Vikings.* New York: Thames & Hudson, 2007.

Hamilton, Edith. *Mythology*. New York: Warner Books, 1942.

Haywood, John. *Viking: The Unofficial Norse Warrior's Manual*. London: Thames & Hudson, 2013.

Lindow, John. *Norse Mythology: A Guide to the Gods, Heroes, Rituals, and Beliefs*. New York: Oxford University Press, 2002.

Oliver, Neil. *The Vikings: A New History*. New York: Pegasus Books, 2013.

Picard, Barbara Leonie. *Tales of the Norse Gods and Heroes*. London: Oxford University Press, 1953.

Richards, Julian D. *The Vikings: A Very Short Introduction*. New York: Oxford University Press, 2005.

Wolf, Kirsten. *Viking Age: Everyday Life During the Extraordinary Era of the Norsemen*. New York: Sterling, 2004.

# WEB SOURCES

Icelandic Saga Database. sagadb.org.

The Norse Mythology Blog. norsemyth.org.

# INDEX

# WANT TO DISCOVER MORE SECRETS OF THE ANCIENT GODS? HERE'S A PEEK AT

# HADES SPEAKS!

## A GUIDE TO THE UNDERWORLD BY THE GREEK GOD OF THE DEAD

# GREETINGS, MORTAL!

**ALLOW ME TO INTRODUCE MYSELF.** I am Hades, king of the ancient Greek underworld, also known as "The God of the Dead," "The Dark Lord," and "Lord of the Place of Darkness." The Romans also called me Pluto, which meant "wealth." And not just because I was "rich" in good looks and charm, but because I had control of all the gold and silver under the earth.

Both the Greeks and the Romans sometimes referred to me as "He Who Must Not Be Named." Yes, that's right. Way before Voldemort and Harry Potter, the ancients were afraid to call my name out loud. They feared that if I heard them, I'd be compelled to drag them down to the underworld.

Honestly, I found this idea quite insulting. I was a *king*. A ruler. I did not bag and tag humans like some evil hunter whenever I heard my name. I let my monstrous minions do that.

You will meet many of them on this tour of my home—monsters such as the multi-headed dog Cerberus and the goat-legged, flame-haired vampire demon Empusa, among many others.

But do not be afraid. They will not touch you, as long as you stay near me. Oh, also, do not eat any of the luscious pomegranates that grow near my palace, because if you do, you will never return to the land of the living. Why rush things, right?

Please, step right up onto my gleaming chariot, led by four giant dark horses. Hold on tight, because when my stallions start racing, we run straight down into a hole in the ground. The noise of the earth opening is spectacular, by the way—kind of like the worst tearing, ripping, crashing sound you can imagine.

What? You'd rather not "fly" into the ground at top speed with me on my chariot? Fine, we'll go the boring way. We'll walk down through one of my many secret cave entrances. (There's one right outside your bedroom.)

Are you ready? I've been waiting for you to visit me for a very long time. . . .

# DOWN, DOWN, DOWN ...

**I HOPE YOU'RE NOT AFRAID** of the dark. If you are, you might consider shutting this book and running outside to play with bubbles in the sunshine. Seriously, my world is the complete absence of light—dark, dim, gloomy, sinister, you name it. No birds chirping in the sunlight around here. Instead, you might find some bloodthirsty bats and even an occasional winged Fury screeching at us.

If you think you can handle it, follow me into this cave entrance. Ahhhh—cold, musty, moldy, wet darkness. The blackness embraces you like a thick

cloak of slime, doesn't it?

I hope you're wearing comfortable shoes, too. It's a long way down. My people—the ancient Greeks—were a strong, hardy lot and would not have been fazed by this long descent into darkness.

The ancient Greeks lived more than 2,500 years ago and were responsible for many of the things you take for granted today, such as democracy, freedom of speech, theater, money, the Olympic Games, and crazy politicians.

In fact, Greece is often called the "cradle of Western civilization." In other words, without us, "you" wouldn't be you. You may thank us for this gift later—preferably with a sacrifice of gold. In my name, if you please.

Anyway, so impressive were my people, the Romans copied just about everything they could steal—er, I mean "borrow"—from us, including Greek architecture, art, philosophy, sculpture, theater, and most importantly, us Greek gods. The Romans renamed us, of course, but we'll talk about those toga-wearing thieves later.

My people lived on mainland Greece and its surrounding islands. Most of Greece is a rocky, mountainous place, which created tough, rugged, adventuresome people. The Greeks sailed into regions unknown (to them, anyway) and established cities in what is now Turkey and even Italy.

While the ancient Greeks were brilliant, they were also a tad warlike. They battled among their many city-states like you and your friends fight for the last piece of candy in the bowl. Athens fought Sparta in a war that lasted decades and got just about every city-state involved in picking sides.

They also fought off invasions from their dreaded enemies, the Persians. But don't get me wrong. I'm not complaining about all that death and destruction. It made my underworld a very busy place.

Aside from their many innovations, however, it is my opinion that the Greek's greatest achievement was—and I say this with all humility—the creation o f us, the Greek gods.

## HOW IT ALL STARTED

The Greeks believed that gods of earth (Gaia) and sky (Ouranos) gave birth to the first gods of the world, the Titans. Kronos, the Titan god of time and age, overthrew his father and took control of the cosmos. His angry parents foretold that one of Kronos's own children would depose him, which is why we gods began as baby food.

Kronos's brilliant plan for getting around the prophecy was to eat his kids as soon as his wife Rhea bore them. See, because we were immortal, he couldn't actually *kill* us. But he could keep us prisoners inside himself. He started by gobbling my sisters—Hestia, Demeter, and Hera. I came next—making me the firstborn son, I should point out—followed by Poseidon.

Our mom, Rhea, was not happy about her husband's baby-eating habit, but she didn't know how to stop him. Finally, by the time my *little* brother Zeus was born, she came up with a plan. (Really, Mom? Nothing occurred to you until the sixth child?)

Rhea gave birth to Zeus in secret, sent him to a faraway cave, and gave Kronos a rock wrapped in a baby blanket to eat instead. Our father swallowed the rock and Zeus got to grow up with beautiful nymph nannies and dancing warriors for entertainment and protection. Talk about spoiled! Meanwhile, the rest us spent our time chillin' in the belly of the beast.

Finally, when Zeus grew up, he made Kronos vomit us out (*ewwww*, I know).Together, my siblings and I defeated dear ol' dad and the other Titans, hurling them deep into the belly of the earth, the lowest level of Tartaros. I call it the pit of punishment.

## WHEN WINNING MEANT LOSING

**W**e won the world! But then we had to figure out how to manage it. As the eldest son, I demanded the lion's share. But baby brother Zeus disagreed. Yeah, he rescued us, and I guess we all owed him one, but still.

We compromised and decided to draw lots. And surprise, surprise—baby brother ended up with all the best bits. Zeus got the earth, the sky, thunder, justice, and all the nations. Poseidon got all the seas and fresh waters, horses, and earthquakes. And me—what did I get? The dead and the dark, dismal underworld. Seriously?

I am convinced my little brother rigged the lottery. He claims that I'm just jealous, but he is completely and utterly wrong. Jealousy is beneath me.

Still, it irks me that you know so little about me, yet you know so much about my *younger* brothers. I bet it's hard for many of you to even conjure up an *image* of me. And why is that? Because statues and paintings of my brothers and sisters were *everywhere* in ancient Greece. But there were hardly any of me. This is an outrage that has bothered me for more than a millennium.

My people built temples to my brothers, Zeus and Poseidon. They built temples to Athena, Artemis, Aphrodite, and many other godlings (minor gods). They even built temples and cult centers devoted to demigod heroes such as Herakles (you know him by his Roman name, Hercules). But they hardly had *any* temples or cult centers devoted to *me*.

Excuse me, but how could there be more shrines devoted to a muscular meathead—Herakles—than temples devoted to the one god they'd hang out with for *eternity*? It wasn't right!

Herakles, by the way, is like homework—useless, boring, and stupid. Yet you will meet him down here many times for the simple reason that I cannot get rid of that club-carrying, lion cloak–wearing muscle man to save my life. He sneaks down here so often that he's become a real pain in the backside. And I mean that literally, as you will see in chapter four.

Also, that scrappy son of Zeus once actually *shot* me in the shoulder with an arrow, right outside my gates. I had to go all the way to Mount Olympus to be treated by the physician to the gods, Paeeon (*pea*-en). Zeus and his out-of-control kids will be the death of me, I swear.

Zeus himself is no saint either, by the way. Not only did he take most of the "good stuff" on the planet, he's constantly meddling in my world. Let me give you an example. Originally, the Olympic Games honored the *dead*. That's right; they started out as funerary contests. The games were designed to appease me by honoring the recently fallen, especially during a war.

Somehow, over the ages, the Olympic Games turned into a massive festival to honor Zeus! Now, no one remembers that they originally began as a way to honor the dead, which means honoring the *king* of the dead—*me*.

Zeus is the little brother from hell, you guys. Seriously.

## HOMER'S BLIND SPOT

**T**he most famous Greek poet, Homer (no, not the cartoon character Homer Simpson—crack open a book, kid!) wrote that my realm was at the "end" of the earth on the western shore of the "river" Oceanus.

He also said it was beyond the gates of the sun and the land of dreams.

Could he have been *any* more vague? That unseeing bard had a blind spot about my world. Just sayin'.

Eventually, almost all ancient Greeks and Romans came to believe that my realm was underground and that it was dark, dank, miserable, and smelly. Now, I ask you, does it stink down here? (Be careful how you answer, kid.) One Greek playwright even described my realm as a "mass of mire" filled with "everlasting dung."

Really? Every poop in the history of the world ends up in "my" house?

I ask you—where's the respect? I mean, this is my *home*, people. How would you like it if I told everyone that your house was filled with poop and stank like rotten eggs, and that no one ever—ever, ever, ever— wanted to come over?

As we get closer to the heart of my world, you might want to memorize the map on the following pages and the path we will take. I highly recommend that you do not get lost. I am not responsible for the actions of my bloodthirsty minions. In case you do get separated from me, go directly to my palace. You'll be safe there. Unless my wife, Persephone (per-*seff*-ah-nee), is in a bad mood, that is.